葛德石
近代中国考察档案文献汇编

3

张 雷 主编

學苑出版社

图书在版编目（CIP）数据

葛德石近代中国考察档案文献汇编．3 / 张雷主编．
—北京 ：学苑出版社，2014.7
ISBN 978-7-5077-4575-7

Ⅰ．①葛… Ⅱ．①张… Ⅲ．①历史地理－档案文献－汇编－中国－近代 Ⅳ．① K928.6

中国版本图书馆 CIP 数据核字 (2014) 第 159474 号

责任编辑：洪文雄　杨　雷
装帧设计：徐道会
出版发行：学苑出版社
社　　址：北京市丰台区南方庄 2 号院 1 号楼
邮政编码：100079
网　　址：www.book001.com
电子信箱：xueyuan@public.bta.net.cn
销售电话：010-67675512　67678944　67601101（邮购）
经　　销：新华书店
印 刷 厂：北京赛文印刷厂
开本尺寸：889×1194　1/16
印　　张：15.25
字　　数：300 千字
版　　次：2014 年 8 月北京第 1 版
印　　次：2014 年 8 月北京第 1 次印刷
定　　价：480.00 元

“我最热爱的是中国”

（总序）

唐晓峰

北京大学 历史地理研究中心

20世纪初年，有一些外国学者凭着强烈的学术意志，来到社会激变的中国。他们宣讲西方学术，探索中国问题，艰苦调查，著书立说，在中国近代学术发展中作出重要贡献。但是由于各种原因，他们之中的许多人都被我们忘掉了。美国大地理学家葛德石（G．B．Cressey）就是其中被忘掉的一位。

1923年，葛德石自欧洲启程，取道北方戈壁荒途来到中国，赴任上海沪江大学（英文名称为Shanghai College）地质与地理系教授，旋任该系主任，组建新式地学教育。他在1926年9月20日写给美国众朋友的公开信中说：“我一个学期要上四门课，总共十一学时，差不多有一百名学生。”“过去两年来，我主要致力于组建工作和安排讲座，从现在起，我应多做些研究了。”在1923年到1929年的六年里，他多次到中国各地进行地理考察，“旅行凡三万哩，除云南、四川、西康、新疆和福建外，足迹所至达二十余省”。当时的中国，军阀混战，社会无序，葛德石的地理考察，因“匪乱和内战，屡为阻障”。例如1926年，“我本想到内蒙古多做些工作，但由于战事而未果。我又打算对滦河做地质考察，此河从蒙古高原流下，至天津北部入海。工作本进展顺利，但到7月13日（不是星期五），我突遭五六个歹徒袭击，工作遂告中断”。

1926至1928年间，葛德石三次油印了一份关于中国地理的书稿。后将书稿完善，配以图表、照片，以 *The Geography of China*《中国地理》为名，交上海商务印书馆印刷。“1932 年即将出版时，逢日本侵入上海，底版被毁，所有图幅及照片全部损失。”此时，葛德石已经返美，在雪城大学（Syracuse University）任地质地理系主任。复经重事编纂，书稿再成，于 1934 年改在纽约出版，名为 *China's Geographic Foundation：A Survey of the Land and its People*（《中国的地理基础》）。

葛德石的书在美国出版后，在中国遂有反响，因受重视，“盗版”书不久问世。据侯仁之师回忆，1936 年先生于燕京大学留校任教，须讲授中国地理学，参考书以葛德石的著作最佳，但原版难求，只能找到非正式翻印的劣版。因一直喜爱此书，先生直到留英期间（40 年代后期），才在英岛购得原版（已然是第八次印刷版），当时的订购单与发票至今与书同为珍藏。

葛德石书原为英文，非正式的中文译本早便流传，且不止一种。直到 1945 年，此书总论部分（前六章）的中译本正式出版，译者是薛贻源，书名为《中国的地理基础》，由开明书店印行。薛氏在译序中说：“总论部分，译者于肄业师大地理系时，承系主任吾师黄海平先生的鼓励课外译读和训诲，即将初稿完成；去冬原著者葛德石教授代表美国国务院访华，于来所就任本所研究员时，得机面请教益，特将译文重加整理出版。”“至于分论部分，系由吾师谌稷如先生译出”，“定名为《中国区域地理》，将另行出版”。所谓分论部分，即第七至二十一章，均为区域地理，包括十五个大区：华北平原、黄土高原、山东辽东热河山地、满洲（东北）平原、满洲东部山脉、兴安岭、中亚草原与沙漠、中央山系、长江平原、四川红壤盆地、江南丘陵、东南沿海、两广丘陵、西南台地、西藏边陲。此分论部分于 1947 年由正中书局出版。

葛德石《中国的地理基础》一书的重要贡献之一，是采用了十五个自然区（见上）的划分方法。此前关于中国的地理著述，多利用已有的政区为区域框架。政区尽管分辨明确，易于指示，但于环境与经济方面，却相当混乱。葛德石指出，“一个农夫生活在河南或在山东的事实，其在地理上的意义，远不及他的农田是在肥沃的平原或在多石的山地。农民更关心的是谷物的适当雨量，而不是省会的名称”。所以对中国景观区域的划分，宜舍弃政治的界线，而依据环境与经济的特征。葛德石的十五区分法，早先在本书的沪江大学油印初稿中便已提出，正式出版时更臻完善。

不过，应该说，舍弃政治界线而取环境特征的中国区域划分方法，并不是自葛德石始，即使在洋人中，1908 年夏之时（L. Richard）的《中国坤舆详志》（*Comprehensive Geography of the Chinese Empire*）就已经用了自然区划法。所以准确地说，葛德石的贡献在于，他的划分更为合理，而其所合之理正是地理学中很要紧的一点，即人与地的关联性。

葛德石的书，以“人类的遗产”一节开篇，他写道：“中国人民生活的根基，深入到土地里面。细心耕种的田园，徒手收获的农作，以及土筑的屋舍，在显示着人与自然的密切联系。”葛德石的地理区域划分，以人地关系特征为指标，观察人如何“渲染”了大地，这最终体现为文化景观。重视文化景观，正是美国地理学的一大特色。一方面是理论传统的引导，另一方面可能产生于同工业化的美国景观的对照。葛德石在中国感受到人与环境的和谐完美：中国“文化景观的种种方面，曾经过了一次进化调和的广泛过程，几乎在每个地方，人们在很久以前，业已尽他所有的工具，来利用自然的富源了。……中国的人生活动已与自然环境完全相适应，我们应用生态植物学的名词，可称之为最理想的‘群落’。”这里，葛德石并非是空发议论，以他在中国“三万哩”的野外观察与情景体验，上述言语应是发自内心。

同样是因为野外考察，他常常发现旧有地理“文本”上的问题。例如在蒙古高原考察时他发现：“许多蒙古地图上都画了不少并不存在的城市，好像作图的人不愿意留出一大块空白的地区。另外，他们参考旅行者的记录，在地图上标满了地名。许多地名是河谷或牧场，也有一些只是井或者不重要的寺庙。其实城市仅仅分布在沙漠的边缘。有一次笔者来到一个地方，在一类标注已成规模的城镇的地图上，这个地方总要被标出来，但那不过是一个电报亭，只住着夫妻俩和一个孩子。还有一次，我用了好几天去找一座在最好的地图上指示的城市，可那座城市早在好几个世纪之前就被成吉思汗毁掉了。”

充分的考察体验与大量的文献整理，构成了写作《中国的地理基础》的基础。在总论中对中国地理形势的宏观把握，在分论中对十五个大区的贴近描述，令一个广袤大国的复杂地理呈现在不同的视野中。科学理性，使本书对中国的优点与劣点并举，在批评方面，并无忌讳。然而，与研究对象的亲近性，又令作者对他所描述的人文大地日渐生情。这是地理学的特点，也是地理学家的特点。我们注意到葛德石在“原序”中脱口而出的一句感慨：因为本书要冷静地对待中国的各方问题，“著者对中国的真诚的友谊，或已难为人知了。”

其实，葛德石“对中国的真诚的友谊”正溢于书表。书中对中国文明的赞美与对中国现代更新的信心，在在可见。葛德石所亲历的中国，正值内乱频发、外患不止的时代，但他在“理解中国”一节中却告诉读者：“目前是不足作为批判中国的代表时期。”“今日中国历史最重要的因素，不是报纸所通常报告的战争和饥馑。经济的、社会的和智力的改进，较之过去军事的和政治的演变，重要得多。中国变动得慢，对于她正有所觉悟的世界新秩序，做完满的适应，也许还需要数十年。而她的结局之为坚忍不拔，那是无可疑的。”

在后来的生活中，葛德石对中国的热爱之情，执著未减。他在雪城的住所，本是一座典型的洋房，却在门廊旁添立了两个中国式的红漆大柱。今天故人已去，但红柱在绿色小丘之间仍十分显眼。葛德石曾说：“中国所表现的艺术和生活的优美，似乎可于北平（北京）得之……住在北平一年，乃是一种世界的最精选的经验。”不知道他选立红漆大柱是否就是受了北京建筑景观的影响。

“二战”期间，葛德石曾任美国国务院驻华文化联络代表，居重庆，与中国地理学家常有来往，并被聘为中国地理研究所兼任研究员。1944 年，中国地理学会成立十周年，美国地理学家协会通过葛德石发来贺文，中国地理学会亦经葛德石回函致谢，信中讲，“葛德石是我们真诚的朋友，他在中国的不算长的时间里，已访过许多地方。他同中国的大多地理学家均有交往，并向我们详细介绍了美国地理学界的工作。”在信上署名的理事有胡焕庸（主席）、翁文灏、竺可桢、涂长望、张印堂、黄国璋、李旭旦（秘书长）等，这都是中国地理学界的泰斗。抗战胜利后，葛德石以个人的名义写了一封热情洋溢的致中国人民的长信，祝愿中国走出战争创痍，抓住历史新机，振兴民族事业。

1949 年春，在里斯本大会上葛德石当选为世界地理学会会长。4 月 7 日应英国著名历史地理学家达比（H.C. Darby）邀请，到利物浦大学做名为“中国的前途（China’s Prospects）”的公开演讲，演讲之后曾由侯仁之先生做答辞。那几天中令侯仁之先生最不能忘怀的是，演讲的第二天，葛德石又被邀做关于苏联的报告，当时葛德石正兼任苏联大地图集顾问，此报告为内部讲座，在报告之先，葛德石特意声明：我今天虽然讲的是苏联，但是“My first love is China（我最热爱的是中国）”。侯先生常常感慨，五十多年过去，这句话依然有声。

1952年，因为在亚洲研究上的卓越贡献，葛德石被授予美国的戴维森勋章。戴维森勋章专为太平洋地区的地理研究而设，葛德石为获此奖项的第一人。1999年，侯仁之先生为获此奖项的第六人。

1954年2月15日，葛德石“以一个从事了三十来年亚洲研究的地理学家的身份”上书艾森豪威尔总统，就当时的美中关系，提出三点建议：一、台湾国民党没有希望再返回大陆，美国必须与共产党打交道。长远战略是将北京与莫斯科分别对待，莫斯科政治上可以影响中国，但要支持北京在经济上独立，不依赖苏联。这是需要的，也是可行的；二、在一年或多一点的时间以后，只要北京遵守最起码的外交礼仪和条约规定，美国就可以承认北京政权。实施程序可以是，先允许日本与北京贸易，然后美国逐渐同中国大陆直接贸易，在北京加入联合国的问题上美国不动用否决权，最后正式承认北京政权。与此同时，对美国公众做宣传教育。三、台湾问题。这是个很麻烦的问题，只要台北与北京都宣称自己代表中国，就不可能有解决办法。美国将继续支持蒋介石，但美国显然也要进行一些调整。

1954年3月12日美国国务院助理国务卿 Walter Robertson 代表总统给葛德石回信，向他申述了美国政府的立场：美国毫无选择地要制裁中国的共产党政权，限制他们同自由世界的贸易，在政治上孤立他们。美国承认台湾的中华民国是中国的合法政权，在联合国代表中国。目前对共产党中国的任何缓和，都会增强他们军备的经济基础，使他们无虑地进攻邻国。承认共产党中国，接受他们在国际社会的合法性，无疑会提高他们的声望。另外，鉴于意识形态的联系与共同的利益，美国看不出在北京与莫斯科之间有任何分歧。美国目前的政策是，逼使北京向苏联索求苏联无法提供的援助，这样就会造成两者关系的紧张。

3月17日葛德石立即给 Robertson 回信，再次申诉自己的观点。他说：我不赞成任何左派或右派的专权。我之所以给总统写信，是希望国际紧张局面能有缓和的一天。只要存在中华人民共和国愿意建立基本的外交关系的可能性，美国就应当有所准备。

用一句俗话说，真不知葛德石欠了我们中国什么，他竟如此“没完没了”地为中国操心。但是，对这样一位差不多半辈子把心放在中国的世界级的大学者，我们现在的中国人倒是太冷淡、太健忘了。回想1987年我在雪城大学过春节。晚会规模很大，有一位美国男子，虽不会讲中国话，却对中国人分外热情，跟每个中国人都打招呼，他必讲的一句话是："My father is Cressey（我父亲是葛德石）。"但 Cressey 是何许人？是他的儿子又如何？他对于中国有什么特别之处？在场的中国人没有一个知道的。归国后，我到上海，找到沪江大学校友会，这个校友会办得很正规，有牌子，有联络处，有专人值守，工作应是很认真的。但是，我查遍了"在校任职外国人名单"，竟没有葛德石的名字。问工作人员，也没听说过。我也查过一些一九四九年以后的中文文献，只在 50 年代的《地理学报》上找到过一篇文章《葛德石反动地理学批判》，文中说："在旧中国葛德石曾经挂着沪江大学'教授'的招牌，干了多年的侦察工作。……葛德石巧于将这些反动观点，包藏在虚伪的关怀、同情与慰勉等好听的言辞当中，偷偷地进行毒害的宣传"，"华尔街走卒"葛德石"'笑里藏刀'的暗害行为，实在较之公开的进攻更为可怕，更是可恨"。20 世纪 50 年代以后，在中国书报很难见到葛德石的名字了。

如此看起来，是我们欠葛德石先生的太多了。问题是，像葛德石这样早年在中国治学，在内心植下对中国的热爱，在 20 世纪 50 年代的风潮中被当作帝国主义政治的陪绑，最后被中国新一代完全忘弃的外国学者，还有不少呢。

不过今日，葛德石的档案有幸被张雷发掘。张雷曾在北大随我读书，后就读于葛德石生前执教终生的美国雪城大学。寒暑几载，他得以遍览该校保存的六十箱葛德石档案，因感慨葛氏的贡献，惜其被埋没，决心在文函图件中重新发现葛德石，并将罕为人知的葛氏中国档案公布于世。档案分别以书信、考察报告、影像的门类编为三册，加上张雷自己撰写的评述葛德石与中国地理学之关系的专著一册，合为四册，一同付梓。

这套书籍，小而言之，是我们对葛德石的回报，是认识葛德石与中国地理学之关系的基础文本；大而言之，是解读近代地理学史以及中美关系史的重要文献，其意义也是不言而喻的。

2014 年 4 月 23 日　于北京五道口嘉园

注：本文最早发表于《读书》2003 年第 12 期，此处为序，略有增删。

总目录

第一卷

葛德石与中国近代地理学

第二卷

葛德石书信档案

第三卷
葛德石在中国考察的报告档案

第四卷
葛德石在中国考察的图像档案

葛德石
近代中国考察档案文献汇编

3
第三卷
葛德石在中国考察的报告档案

张　雷　主编

目录

前 言

葛德石一生曾三次前来中国考察，其中第一次是1923—1929年，在上海沪江大学任教期间，侧重对我国西北地区和江浙地区考察。第二次是1934年，葛德石受国民政府邀请考察了江浙地区的土地利用情况。第三次是1943—1944年，葛德石作为美国国务院派遣的访华教授，考察了重庆、昆明等中国西南地区。

在三次中国考察中，葛德石均撰有相应报告。这些材料构成葛德石的著作《中国的地理基础》以及《亚洲之地与人》的基础。但是葛德石成书时对这些报告有取有舍，读者难以从中窥见全貌，故本次整理葛氏档案文献时全文收录葛氏档案中所藏的报告，并采取影印的方式整理，不做原文献的全文翻译，以期最大限度地呈现这些档案的原貌。

葛德石的报告对现今社会仍具有重要价值。例如葛德石的青海湖考察报告，记录了葛德石从鄂尔多斯，取道甘肃，考察青海湖的路程及沿途景观，是了解20世纪20年代我国西北地区的重要地理文献。而葛德石的滦河遇险可窥见当时地理考察之艰难。沪江大学地理地质系的报告则是了解民国教会大学地学系的一篇重要资料。1944年葛德石的考察报告涵盖教育、工业以及政治等，是了解战时中国及中美关系的重要资料。1945年之后的报告则反映葛德石作为一个地理学家，对二战之后的中美关系的观察和解读。本次对葛德石中国考察报告文献的整理，基本囊括葛氏档案所藏的考察报告，并且以葛德石在中国的考察时间为顺序进行整理，以期最大限度地呈现这些档案的历史脉络。

第三卷
葛德石在中国考察的报告档案

第一章（1924–1928）

1924—1929 年，在沪江大学地质与地理系任教期间，葛德石深感中国地质与地理资料严重不足，因此，他决定利用每年寒暑假，选取特定区域进行综合考察，收集相关材料。科学地理考察的兴起对中国近代地理学的发展具有重要的意义，一方面它为近代地理学研究积累了大量可靠的一手资料，另一方面也改变了传统地理学足不出户的研究方法。葛德石在 20 年代末就已经完成了系统的中国地质地理考察。中国考察成就了葛德石，三万英里的行程成为葛德石解读中国地理的基石，为葛德石的中国地理研究做好了准备。

1924 年，葛德石结束在华北协和华文学校的汉语学习之后，开始中国地理考察。其中最重要的考察是 1925 年夏，进行的蒙古、甘肃、青海考察。而葛德石 1926 年滦河考察之险，反应了当时地理考察的艰辛。除了考察之外，葛德石还主持沪江大学地质地理系，现存报告一篇，可见沪大地质地理系当年概况。

1925年
青海湖考察报告

"KOKO NOR"

(An account of a unaccompanied journey across northwestern China to the borders of Mongolia and Tibet)

George B. Cressey Ph. D.
Professor of Geology
Shanghai College
Shanghai, China

KOKO NOR

There is a fascination about the unknown which drives men out to the ends of the earth. Those who do not feel it smile at the wanderer and think him foolhardy, but to others what some call impossible is only the more alluring. To many people, China consists of only a narrow strip along the coast and up the Yangtze. To be sure the maps show towns and provinces away from the treaty ports, but this outer darkness is largely unknown and certainly uninviting. All China is just the same, anyway, so why should one travel into the interior and invite acquaintance with the bandits who are so fond of foreign devils these days.

China's northwest is one of the least known and most sparsely populated sections of the country. On the north are the deserts of Mongolia, while to the west rise the mountains and plateaus of Tibet. Between them lie the provinces of Kansu and Shensi, a gateway between Chinese Turkestan and the plains of eastern China. The region is one totally different from what the tourist sees in Shanghai or Peking. Rice and bamboo are unknown. There are no canals and very few rivers. In place of the crowding millions one may travel an entire day and scarcely see half a dozen people. The general layout of the land has been described by an occasional traveller, but until railroads are eventually built the country will remain undeveloped and largely unexplored.

My friends in Peking were distressed when they heard that I proposed to travel through this region entirely alone, and live off the country. Everyone was sure that I would die of some horrible disease for doctors are a months journey apart, or that if by some miracle I lived and survived the hot weather, the bandits would surely make way with me. These warnings, however, made me only the more anxious to see if the country really was so dangerous. I had travelled a thousand miles across Mongolia the summer before without great hardship, and people had been even more emphatic in their forecasts on that occasion.

The main caravan road to Kansu starts at Sianfu in the southern part of Shensi. This is a much travelled highway, but inasmuch as I was anxious to see the edge of Mongolia on the way west, I decided instead to cross central Shansi and northern Shensi, and follow what trails I could find. Six hours south of Peking on the Hankow railroad is the junction station of Shih chia chwang. Here a narrow guage line leaves the plain of north China and climbs through pretty mountain valleys to Taiyuanfu the capital of the province of Shansi.

Between Taiyuanfu and Fenchow lies the broad plain of the Fen River, and over the modern automobile road a public bus maintains an every other day schedule. Here at Fenchow was the starting point for my journey by pack animal out into the unknown. Since few travellers ever enter Kansu by this route, I was unable to find a multeer who knew the road for more than a few stages. Thru the help of friends I secured two good mules which were ordinarily used in carrying mail. As I bid these friends farewell at the city gate, I little realized that their cheery good wishes would be the last English that I would hear for 36 days.

On leaving the Fenchow plain, the road to the west abruptly plunges into a maize of canyons among the loess hills, and with equal suddenness I was engulfed in a new world. Perhaps my confidence in thus starting out on such an adventure was in part due to a false security. The few maps which I carried showed everywhere a generous sprinkling of roads and towns. How was I to know that, apparently, many of them had been put in by some kindly cartographer who had heard of China's teeming millions and so imagined that the whole country was regularly spaced with villages. This confidence in ~~[illegible]~~ supposedly accurate geography and my blissful ignorance of the unpleasant side of Chinese travel were soon changed. The red line which we were following on the map entirely neglected to go in the same direction which the dusty trail actually went. They both ended at the same town that night, but even thisagreement was soon at an end. Chinese food around Peking is not at all bad, and there are usually quiet temples for the traveller. Mot so in Shansi and even less farther west; and much of the glamour of the distant unknown fades on too close examination.

I had been somewhat at a loss as to what kind of equipment would be most needed. I was anxious to travel as lightly as possible, and while a tent would have been valuable on a few occasions, I managed without it. On one mule was a cot, bedding role, and such equipment as was necessary for the geological work which I planned to do. These made a light load so that I could ride a part of the time. On the other mule was a small food box for day to day supplies and two strong boxes in which were my few stores. These consisted of canned milk, sugar, chocolate, raisins, Kodak films and a few presents.

For the most part I lived off the country. In almost every village eggs could be bought for a cent or less, and towards the end of the summer vegetables were generally available. Rice is almost unknown in the northwest, millet and wheat being the staple cereals instead. The former is eaten as a porridge while wheat flour is used for mien or noodles and for round four inch cakes of bread. This bread is quite good when fresh but hardens to a rock after two or three days. Meat was scarcer than I had anticipated, and altho pork was sometimes available it was hardly to be recommended. Villages are often several days journey apart and I usually had to carry supplies between them as the occasional inns have no food on hand.

Chinese inns have a well deserved reputation for filth, and I had hoped that it would be possible to camp outside. On account of feed for the mules it was impossible to be far from an inn, and on many scores it developed that the only way to travel rapidly was simply to submit to the system. I usually managed to obtain a room to myself, tho it was often one occupied by a dozen coolies who had to find accomodations elsewhere. Flies and virmin are inevitables, and there is no de luxe class available.

Between Fenchow and the Yellow River, the road runs over low mountain country thickly covered with loess. The rainfall is so slight that hillside cultivation is seldom practical and all the houses are confined to the valley bottoms where small streams make irrigation possible. For much of

-5-

the distance, the mule trail parallels the new American Red Cross auto road to the Yellow River. Despite the nearly 2000 miles of modern roads in the province, there are still few automobiles and on this road several bridges have been washed out so that traffic was limited to a few broad tired carts.

The Yellow River forms a natural boundary between the provinces of Shansi and Shensi. Because of several small rapids there is almost no navigation. Where I crossed it the river is quite turbulent and there are large stationary waves which make the passage decidedly thrilling. The mules were very skittish about getting into the ferry, and it was only after considerable beating and shouting that they were persuaded to jump into the small boat.

Northern Shensi is quite arid and those few valley bottoms which are capable of irrigation are largely being used for the raising of opium poppy. The tax from the opium is one of the largest sources of revenue for the local militarists and all thru Shansi and Kansu the farmers have been compelled to plant it. In some districts two-thirds of the irrigated land is thus used.

There are many outcrops of coal seams and a few native mines. I was anxious to see something of mining methods and so persuaded one group of miners to let me go underground. There was no ladder in the sixty foot shaft, and so they tied a rope around my waist and let me down hand over hand. At the bottom were three radiating tunnels extending out some 200 feet to where half a dozen men were digging out the coal. These workings were less than three feet high and the men lay on their sides and undercut the two ten inch seams with small picks. There was no timbering and accidents are rather common. The operation of these mines was most primitive, and the expense of shipping the coal by donkey back limited the distribution to a small area.

Ten days west of Fenchow I reached the Great Wall and the Ordos Desert. The Ordos is a southward projection of Inner Mongolia which causes the Wall to make a big swing to the southwest. On the north and west of the Desert flows the Yellow River, and within this area lies a sandy waste peopled only by a few nomadic Mongol tribes. Along the eastern border Chinese colonists are pushing across the wall, but even in the most favored localities dry farming has only limited possibilities. Wherever the soil been disturbed by plowing, the high winds have whipped up sand dunes which gradually advance across the country, burying trees and farms. In some places the Great Wall itself is being covered. It is impossible to penetrate far into this vast sandy desert without a well equipped caravan and supplies of water. I was anxious, however, to see something of conditions outside the Wall and determined to travel as far as possible.

On the maps which I carried there was prominently indicated a town in the southern Ordos by the name of Borobalgasson. One German map entitled it "Trummer der Stade", and from the radiating roads and the bold type, I imagined that it would serve as a good point to buy supplies and study Mongol life.

-7-

When I reached the Great Wall, I therefore inquired about this city. Repeated questioning failed to elicit any information, however. I thought that quite possibly my pronunciation of the Mongol name might be unrecognizable, so I set out northward. For the first few miles there was a little cultivation, but soon all sign of a trail vanished and we entered a tract of bare sand dunes. Even the occasional Mongols whom we met failed to recognize the name of the town, and two days later after reaching the locality where the town should have been, I was forced to give it up as a mystery. Where there should have been a city, I had found only a barren waste of shifting sand. Later I learned that Borobalgasson had been destroyed by Kubalai Khan in the thirteenth century. So incomplete is our ~~knowledge~~ geographic knowledge of the Ordos that this town is prominently indicated on most maps of China, even the most recent. In several sections of the Ordos I was the first foreigner who had ever visited the region, and even in areas where a few white men have been, almost none have been concerned with maps.

During the week which I spent in the southern Ordos, I saw only a little of the nomadic Mongol life which I had anticipated. The few people who inhabit the region have settled down in Chinese style houses and in the change in their mode of life they have deteriorated physically. In a few places near the Wall there are lower depressions which are covered with bunch grass and a profusion of yellow hyacinths, purple daisies, and other wild flowers. Most of the region, however, is covered with bare sand. The poverty of the land is in impressive contrast to the glory of the evening sky. Other regions may have finer sunsets but these have a special quality in the inky blackness of some of the clouds, due perhaps to the 4000 feet elevation. The sky itself was tinged with brilliant shades of gold, burnt orange, robbins egg blue, and royal purple.

Travel across the sand dunes was very fatiguing. The weather was extremely hot and the glare from the sand was blinding. On all sides there were only rolling waves of sand. Even from the crests of the highest nothing was to be seen but billow upon billow of bare yellow sand; not a bush or blade of grass; no sign of a trail; and not even distant mountains by which to guide. To add to this desolation, on several days there were blinding sand storms. The wind whistled and shrieked. The air became a thick cloud of sand, and I could scarcely see the ground at my feet. The mules were tied together so that they would not become separated and lost. When there was a lull in the storm we staggered forward, but in a moment screaming blasts of sand would almost carry us off our feet. There was no shelter and the muleteer had spells of abject terror. Without a guide and without knowledge of waterholes or the country ahead, it is a marvel that we did come out anywhere. Travel northward became more and more difficult, and without feed for the mules and with little water for ourselves, we were forced to turn back to the south.

Even when we returned to what was called the main road my troubles were not over. A few days later one of the mules became sick, and the muleteer was obliged to return to

Fenchow. Even tho he had proved to be very lazy and helpless, it had nevertheless been a comfort to have a companion. From here westward I had to hire animals from place to place, and during the rest of the summer had twelve different sets of muleteers or carters. Many pages in my journal are filled with comments on these men, and by no means all of the observations are complimentary. Lazy, timid, unresourceful; I certainly found many of them to be a pretty poor sort. It is not without reason that the Chinese have a saying - "Carters, boatmen, inn keepers, yamen runners; all, even those without fault, should be shot".

Northern Kansu from the Great Wall to the main Sianfu - Lanchow - Turkestan highway is a semi-arid region of brown plains and hills. Near the Great Wall are several salt lakes, and only in a few fertile valleys toward the south is agriculture really profitable. Millet, wheat, and opium are the chief crops.

A week after leaving the Ordos, I reached Haicheng in northern Kansu. Haicheng is the center of a large Mohammedan district, and I found the people a most interesting racial mixture. The Mohammedans are not, as so many imagine, merely Chinese with a particular religion but are of a distinct race. Kansu has been the gateway for most of the migrations into China from the west, and tucked away in its mountains are people of marked Persian, Turkish, and Jewish types, as well as Mongoloid forms strikingly similar to the North American Indians. The Mohammedans of Kansu have a distincly Near East appearence.

The women do not bind the feet, as is still the almost universal custom with the Chinese of the northwest. In place of the conventional Chinese blue, their clothes are colored green and red and purple. Fifty years ago the Mohammedans killed fifteen million Chinese in a great rebellion, and there is still much enemity today.

I had been anxious to visit Haicheng to study the effects of the great earthquake of 1920 which caused such great landslides. These wiped out many towns and resulted in a loss of life which official Chinese estimates place at 246,000. For two days before reaching Haicheng I had seen minor effects such as ruined farmhouses or the caving in of the common vaulted rooms cut in the loess, but there had been nothing of any great magnitude, In the city, however, the effects were very evident. The city wall had been entirely destroyed and most buildings thrown down by the intense earth tremors. Out of a former population of at least 15,000 only 900 people remained, and desolation was on every hand. Fortunately all buildings in this part of China are built merely of sun dried bricks or of pounded earth so that there is no fire danger and with patience they are readilly rebuilt.

Haicheng lies just to the east of one of the several north suth ranges of mountains which characterize northern Kansu. Between these higher areas of old igneous rocks lie basins and lower hills of loess and unconsolidated sands. The mountains are bordered by thrust faults of recent origin and it is along some of these that the movement took place on the evening of December 16, 1920. The fault plane nowhere extends to the surface, but the slips which occured resulted in the most disastrous earthquake in history. As I left Haicheng and crossed the mountains to the west, I found that all traces of destruction ceased as soon as I reached bed rock. Old walls and even houses of weak construction were not cracked whereas three or four miles away everything had been destroyed. Here as at Yokahama and San Francisco is an illustration of the fact that it is the soft unconsolidated land which is most sharply vibrated whereas on hard rock the movement is more gentle.

On the other side of the mountains in the bare loess hills I suddenly discovered even more stupenduous evidence. I first came upon several landslides where masses of earth had slid down from the hills making a lake a quarter of a mile long. Here and there on the hillside were open crevasses and the slopes showed billows where the soil had flowed like tar. Nearby the evidence was even more striking and was on a vast scale. On every side were huge ampitheatres where half a hill had slid into the valley. The entire aspect of the land had been altered by vast landslides, The Chinese were literally correct when they said that the mountains had walked. From one hill top I counted forty of these great slides, each several hundred yards wide and a half to two miles long. The earth displaced totals many cubic miles. Even where the ground had not rolled away there were open fissures, and scarcely any slope was unaffected. The surface of the slides was in the wildest confusion. Trees were tossed about and where two lines of flow met, blocks of the hard surface soil were piled into heaps twenty five feet high resembling pressure ridges in ice floes.

¶ In one valley a series of slides had crashed down one side and piled up in a ridge four miles long against the opposite slope. In one instance this avalanche stopped within two feet of a doorway. All people living in the valley bottoms must have been instantly wiped out as the avalanches thundered down on them during the night. On the borders of the worst area I saw ruined houses where the brick beds or kangs had broken thru in just the outline of some sleeper who had been let down into the smouldering fire beneath. Death and destruction were everywhere, and the occasional farmer pitifully attempting to level out a little field emphasized the desolation.

Thru the earthquake country all signs of a trail were blotted out in the changed landscape and travel was difficult. The ground resembled the confused pack ice of the Polar Sea. Even away from these regions there were no well travelled trails, for the population in this semi-arid district has always been small.

Shortly after leaving the center of the earthquake area, I reached the main Sianfu - Lanchow highway east of Huining. Along this great trade route, the most important cart road in all China, moves a constant stream of two wheeled carts, pack animals and foot travellers, and in two hours I saw more traffic than I had seen in the past two weeks. Four days later I arrived in Lanchow, the capital of Kansu. Since leaving Fenchow 36 days previously, I had travelled 2440 li, or 800 miles. The last few days I had been moving particularly rapidly, and had covered 165 miles in five days, all of it on foot. The luxury of a rest and good food in Lanchow were thus most decidedly welcome.

Lanchow is located on the right bank of the Yellow River which here flows thru a broad valley in contrast to the rapids and canyons both above and below the Lanchow plain. It is a city of half a million, and the stores are surprisingly well stocked. Curio shops sell little porcelain budhas "made in Japan", and one would scarcely know that it was not on a railroad. An auto road to Sianfu is now under construction, and until the railroad is built will serve to bind this metropolis of the northwest with the coast. Perhaps the most surprising sight is the fine steel bridge across the river, built by an American. This is one of the three bridges across the Yellow River, the others being railroad structures on the Plain of North China.

Southwestern Kansu beyond Lanchow proved to be the most prosperous part of the province which I had seen. The elevation is everywhere over a mile so that the climate is entirely suited to Western fruits and vegetables. The apricots especially were as fine as any I have ever tasted. Here as in the north, the irrigated valley bottoms are largely devoted to the raising of opium poppy. In contrast to northern Kansu, however, the hillsides are more often green, and the snow capped mountain spurs of Tibet frequently form a part of the landscape.

The route which I followed led south from Lanchow to Titao and thence northwest through Hochow and Hsunhwa to the great Tibetan monastary of Kumbum. Even more than the region around Haicheng, this is a great center for Mohammedans, and Hochow is their Oxford with many important schools. Altho supplies of food in the smaller villages were none too abundant, the larger towns had good inns and I usually fared quite well. The main roads in the province are all lined with trees, and their shade and the delightful weather made travel very pleasant. We had rain almost every day, but it seldom interfered with travel and was a welcome change from the burning heat of the north.

Beyond Titao the road entered the mountains and became only a narrow mule trail. Several times we crossed passes over 12,000 feet in height, and altho they were clear from snow, there were splendid views of rugged snow peaks a few thousand feet higher. The trail over these ridges usually followed rushing torrents to their source and then struck straight up the side of the mountain. Climbing was difficult enough in any case, but when I walked more than fourty miles one day in going over the steepest of these crests, it was about enough.

At the summit of every pass were clusters of Tibetan prayer sticks, placed there by devout travellers to appease the spirits of the mountain. All thru Mongolia it is common to see piles of stones at the divides, but these were the first of the Tibetan corollary which I had discovered. After leaving Lanchow I had begun to see a few Tibetan travellers, and beyond the first pass between Titao and Hochow I found a number of settlements. In these clumps of prayer sticks were about a hundred pieces of wood, one inch in diameter and six to ten feet long, stuck into a three foot mound of stones. Some were plain, but most were painted and had tufts of wool stuck on them. At the top of these poles were three gaudily decorated boards some three inches wide and two feet long fastened lengthwise like the feathers on an arrow. I was anxious to obtain a set of these boards, but when the muleteer and a passing traveller saw that I had taken a set, they were in abject terror. They assured me that I would be killed by the first Tibetan whom we should meet, and that even if undiscovered, my act wuld bring great misfortune on the morrow. The muleteer flatly refused to move a step until they were thrown away. I was standing several feet away and it was in the dusk of a late afternoon, so that when I made a swing he did not know that I merely stuck them under my coat.

At Hsunhwa I crossed the Yellow River for the second time during the summer. West of Fenchow it had proved exciting enough, but here we had all the thrills of an ocean voyage. The river was only fifty yards wide, but we floated downstream half a mile before the crew could get the makeshift boat to the other side. From here on the trail was even more obscure, and we frequently lost our way in rolling upland moors. After several days we reached the great Lamasary of Kumbum with its 3600 monks, and here I spent some time resting and visiting the temples. This is the most important center in northeastern Tibet, and pilgrims come from great distances.

When I had first planned on the summers wanderings I had thought of Lanchow as my objective. I later decided to include southwestern Kansu, and now that I was actually as far as Kumbum it seemed a great misfortune if I should return without having a glimpse of Lake Koko Nor in northeastern Tibet. I had heard of its great beauty, and the chance of really getting into Tibet was worth a strenuous attempt. Someone has said that every fool with the wanderlust heads for Tibet as soon as he gets loose. That may be true, but at least the possibility of reaching Koko Nor had not occured to me while in Peking and I had deliberatly left behind the maps for everything west of Lanchow. The decision was as good as made when it was first evident that I might possibly make it, tho I did not say it out loud until we reached Kumbum.

Altho Kumbum is actually within the traditional boundary of Tibet, the political boundary is today farther west. To reach Koko Nor it is necessary to reenter a corner of China and follow up the Sining River to Tangar, the westernmost Chinese town and just beyond the old boundary. The next day after leaving Kumbum I reached the gorge of the Sining and high up on a cliff saw carved in the rock the words "The throat to Tibet". I was actually in the forbidden and mysterious land, and visions of the few who had penetrated before me swept across my mind. To be sure, one step across the boundary did not suddenly change the landscape for I had not yet reached the great plateau. Nevertheless I had arrived, and no matter what happened I could put down at least one achievement. I was now two months journey from the coast, and had

-17-

travelled without servant, guide, or campanions other than mule drivers. I had several times had a bit of dysentary and there had been frequent reports of nearby bandits. The worst was still to come, but so was the best and the net result proved to be greatly worth while.

Tangar is the starting point for one of the main highways from China Proper to Lhassa, and had I been a few months earlier I should have seen the long caravans of yak heading up the valley to the south. But altho the Lhassa traders were already far along on their two months journey across the bleak plateau, there still were other smaller caravans which I saw as we started out on that highroad. My muleteer had been quite positive in his refusal to venture beyond Tangar, but the smooth talk of a so-called guide and interpreter whom I secured there finally persuaded him. A few miles beyond this last Chinese city is a little Tibetan style bridge across the stream. I doubt if after it there is another bridge for hundreds of miles to the southwest. After crossing this rude structure, the road leaves the valleys which drain into China and mounts the plateau which here slopes inward toward Koko Nor. By evening we reached the divide and after crossing a broad saddle soon caught a glimpse of the matchless lake, a glistening silver ribbon far out to the west.

If the gorge of the Sining had brought no abrupt change in scenery, here at least was contrast. Here there were no more trees in the valleys, and the mountains at once became more snow covered and majestic. Despite this change and the thrill of the occasional yak caravans laden with unknown treasures from the interior, I was by no means prepared for the glimpse of the lake. It was about five o'clock that we first saw it; just a sparkling sheen at the foot of distant snow clad peaks. The lake itself is 10,700 feet above sea level and is surrounded by encircling mountains which rise several thousand feet higher. It is not a large lake as lakes go, being only 65 miles from east to west and 50 miles wide. Its setting, nevertheless, makes it one of the great sights of the world. The clearness of the sky at this altitude imparts a very deep blue color to the water, so that its name in Chinese, Mongolian and Tibetan all mean "blue lake". Koko Nor, as it is commonly known in English is the Mongolian name, while the Chinese call it Ching Hai and the Tibetans know it as Tsong Nong Pu.

The Tibetans have a most curious legend as to the origin of the lake. It seems that years ago a sovreign in Lhassa thrice failed in attempting to construct a large shrine. His wise men were unable to discover the reason for the failure of the foundations until one of them after years of wanderings came to the valley of the Koko Nor. Here he came upon an old nomad who accidentally revealed the secret. It seemed that underneath Lhassa there was a great sea, and that it was into this that the buildings had sunk. In punishment to the old man for thus telling the secret, the gods decreed that this subterranean ocean should break out in his valley and destroy his tents and flocks. That night the fountains of the deep broke forth and formed what is now Lake Koko Nor. But the flood once started might have covered the whole earth had not a great bird brought a huge rock from the Nan Shan Mountains and dropped it into the lake just where the opening was. This rock may still be seen as an island in the center of the lake. On it there is a little monastary where those who would obtain great merit go to spend a season. Since there are no trees in this region, there are no boats and the pilgrims can cross only during the winter on the ice, being forced to remain on the island during the summer.

A few miles beyond the divide we came upon ~~the ruins of~~ an old city now entirely in ruins, and outside of it by a little stream we found a temple named Ha Shun Miao. Here one or two roofs were still in place and we found shelter for the night. In the main hall, what to my delight should I discover but the crude painting of a great rock falling into stormy waters below. Here apparently was the place where the thankful used to gather to commemorate the fortunate cessation of the threatened flood.

Koko Nor is now a salt water lake, but th the southeast is a low saddle, perhaps six or eight hundred feet above the present lake level thru which it seems probable that the lake overflowed during the Pleistocene or Glacial period. At the time when much of North America and Europe were covered with ice, Central Asia was also ~~doubtless~~ mush colder than at present. While the precipitation was ~~also~~ doubtless ~~hhhh~~ greater than now, there was not enough snow or rainfall to form an ice sheet, and the chief effect was an increase in the size of the many inland lakes. The water of Koko Nor is only slightly saline and probably represents the accumulation during post glacial time since it has ~~had an~~ ceased to have an outlet. Around its shores is a broad gently sloping sand belt, still marshy in places, from which the water has but recently receded. Evaporation exceeds the inflow, and the size of the lake is slowly on the decline. Along the eastern border of the lake this sand flat is six to eight miles wide and is covered in most places with bunch grass. Just back from the lake I found some fresh water lagoons, and here we camped.

I spent three days beside the Blue Sea. Clear, bracing days under a bright but not uncomfortably hot sun; with matchless orange sunsets in a cloudless sky; and cold nights under the brightest stars beneath which I've ever slept. What more could be asked as the climax of a summer. Superb mountains, a crystal lake, and high adventure in a mysterious land where perhaps not a dozen other Americans have ever been. Far out in the lake I could see the island of the monastary, and a few days later as we left the region by a high mountain pass I could just make out the distant western shore. Wild rabbits and fleet antelope were abundant while overhead were many geese. The beach was of clean white sand, and the water tho cool was fine for swimming. Some day when railroads are built and travel becomes simple, people in Shanghai may run up to Koko Nor for a week end, but I was thankful that the day of real estate agents and summer villas was still far distant. Half

-21-

the charm of Koko Nor lies in its solitude. The peacefulness of the azure lake and the grandeur of the distant mountains cast a spell over one which is not soon forgotten.

Tucked away in a little side valley and yet within sight of the lake lies the monastary of Yun ji gum pa. Monastaries are found everywhere in Tibet, often in the least expected situations. This one had only sixty lamas and the curious thing was that it was all in tents. Thruought most of Tibet the people are real nomads moving about in their black tents according to the grass for their flocks, and building no permenant structures. The monastaries are thus almost the only fixed settlements and are commonly in buildings of very substantial construction. Yun ji gum pa was an exception, and altho it had been located in exactly this spot for something like four hundred years, there were no buildings.

I had heard rumors of the place while in Tangar, but on asking my guide whether a group of tents we found one day were the monastary, he was quite insistant that we should not venture near them. He assured me that it was only a settlement of nomads whose fierce dogs would surely give us trouble. Since Tibetan nomads sounded equally interesting, and I was at the time ignorant of their dogs, I insisted on turning aside. Fortunately we somehow missed the dogs and discovered that it was really the monastary. After being inspected by one lama after the other, I was at last ushered into the tent of the Abbot. I found him to be a simple and approachable man, and quite surprised to see me. We talked awhile, he in rather broken Chinese but probably no worse than mine, and then he assigned one of the monks to take me on a tour of inspection about the place.

Altho most of the inhabitants of the Koko Nor region are Tibetans, a few are Mongolians, and the tents of the monastary were representative of each. The typical Tibetan tent is of black cloth made from yak hair and is held up by four poles at the corners with additional supports if large. The Mongolian tent or yurt is made of white felt and covers a circular lattice frame work. These were the only yurts which I saw in the neighborhood of the lake, but the black tents did not differ from the score or more of others which we came upon from time to time. Toward the front of the group of tents was a large black one, perhaps twenty by thirty feet which served as both chanting hall and kitchen. Here the lamas met each morning, and often at other times during the day, to go thru their incantations before drinking tea. There were a number of rugs on the floor and on them were lying various objects used in the worship: prayer wheels, bells of different sizes, small statues of Buddhas wrapped in yellow silks, scrolls, and "books" of the sheets of paper on which are printed various sacred writings.

Even more noticeable, however, was the grease and smell which is as typical of the Tibetans as the nomadic condition of their life. Their food includes much fat mutton and butter, and since it is eaten with the fingers and these are wiped on the clothing, the latter soon acquire a permenant odor and shine.

In addition the temple lights burn butter and as they drip badly the posts to which they are attached soon become coated. There were several lamas in this combination of dining hall and temple, and as I squatted on the floor and visited with them, they presently offered me some food. I have forgotten now, but it was probably mutton; I well remember though that it was only with [redacted] considerable courage that I ate a courteous portion.

There were perhaps two score tents in all, and after seeing the best of them and greatly amusing some of the monks by taking their pictures, I returned to the tent of the Abbot. By this time he was attired in reception robes and seated on the floor of the tent behind a little ten inch table. I sat down opposite him and he preceeded to show me his treasures, a collection of old picture post cards. They were all very much thumbed and were doubtless some which pilgrims or wandering merchants had picked up during the course of many years. A few were scenes from different cities in Europe or America, but most of them were floral cards of birthday wishes or "Greetings from Smithville, wish you were here" and the like. They apparently had little meaning to him, and how was he to know which side up to hold them, having never seen skyscrapers or bathing girls. These pictures and various other nick nacks having been presented for my approval, the next item was tea.

Tibetan tea is served in wooden bowls and is a steaming hot grey colored beverage made of sour milk, salt, brick tea, and butter. All Tibetan milk is sour because the containers are never washed, while brick tea is a compressed block of black tea; leaves, stems, dirt and all from which tea is shaved as desired. An attendant brought in two bowls for us and placed them on the stand between us. The Abbot than pulled out a little drawer in the table in which were several lumps of butter, some of which were none too fresh. Taking one of the lumps in his hand, a hand which certainly had not been washed for many moons, he squeezed off two goodly portions and put them into our bowls of tea. Next came a handful of parched barley flour and, thus concocted, we proceeded to drink the result. It was more like a gruel than tea, and I was surprised to find the taste less unpleasant than I had feared. Later on came little lumps of cheese the size of peanuts and various other delicacies. The tea was so hot that I could scarcely drink it, but if I was slow about sipping my bowl, it was at once thrown out and a new bowl prepared, apparently on the supposition that I was refusing to drink it because it had gotten cold. The Abbot was quite pleasant and seemed genuinely glad that I had visited him. Doubtless he is not used to entertaining foreigners often; in fact he [redacted] spoke of only two others who had ever visited the monastary.

Some days later I left the lake from near the north eastern corner, crossing a high divide to get back to Tangar from the west. The last sight of the lake as I saw it on a late afternoon was perhaps the finest view of all. The sun in the west set the whole body of water aflame and every part of it was radiant with a flashing sparkle. The pass was free from snow but all about us and in the mountains around the lake were many patches of snow. It had rained a little as we scrambled up the pass, but from the summit the view was clear and the country spread out below us in a broad panorama. The broad grass covered plain could be traced almost around the lake, and next to the water with its tracery of small waves was the white sandy beach with here and there an area of bare sand dunes. In one or two valleys near the plain I could just see a few small white dots representing the flocks of some nomad whose black tents I could faintly make out thru the binoculars.

I had found these nomads to be simple childlike people, rather friendly and exceedingly curious. Everything that I had was of interest to them, my collapsable tripod taking chief place. They would feel of my white skin and laugh at my light hair, and seemed to enjoy me hugely. We could not talk to each other, but there was the universal sign language. Perhaps the chief obstacle to making contacts with them are their fierce dogs, of which every group of tents has at least three. These are huge powerful beasts, even larger than the savage mongolian dogs which are the scavengers of Urga in Outer Mongolia. These Tibetan dogs have a hoarse bark which suggests that the visitor would do well to remain mounted until someone from the tents sends them sulking away with a sharp command. To kill a Tibetan dog is a serious offense, and the owner of the dog must be given the price of a yak. Hence the only recourse is to throw them some food and trust for the speedy arrival of their master.

Even tho it was the middle of the summer, the Tibetans were still wearing their heavy felt clothing which usually consisted of a loose one-piece robe with a girdle around the waist. If the day were very warm, they took one arm out of the sleeve and left the shoulder bare, but the days when it was really warm were uncommon. The nights were actually cold, and despite sweaters, wool shirts, and three blankets, I had still been chilly. My poor muleteer had failed to bring any extra bedding and despite some things which I gave him, the poor fellow almost froze. He had been almost petrified with fear ever since we left Kumbum, and the cold of these Tibetan nights did not serve to increase his love of the country. He talked and acted as though he were sure that this was the edge of the world, and if he were not killed by the Tibetans he was sure that they would steal his animals. Every day he repeatedly implored me to return before it was too late and several times when I had gotten out of sight, I found that he had turned the mules around and started back. Scared as the sailors of Columbus, it was only by the direst of threats that I kept him with me. At night I slept with all of his bags under my cot and my pistol under my pillow. Like so many of the muleteers, he was quite satisfactory on the main trails but once out of his environment he was entirely helpless.

Tibet may be represented on the five colored Chinese flag, but no Chinese dare venture very far into that country without military protection. It developed that the guide whom I had hired at Tangar spoke no Tibetan and had never been where we went after all. He was less afraid than the mulateer but was very tricky and at times decidedly nervous. When we returned to Tangar, I rather reluctantly gave each of them a little bonus, but they were already so delighted at seeing things Chinese again that they were as happy as children without it. Even before we reached the inn, they began telling everyone along the street of their adventures and how brave they had been. No doubt their courage and daring will continue to form the subject of many a conversation for some years to come as they slowly smoke their pipe and relate their experiences to eager listeners.

(About 7100 words)

George B. Cressey,
Professor of Geology,
Shanghai College,
Shanghai, China

1926年
滦河考察遇险报告

2

DR. CRESSEY RELATES LWAN RIVER ADVENTURE

Letter From Peitaiho Tells Of Ill-Fated Scientific Expedition Ruined By Midnight Attack By Bandit Gang; Magistrate Promises Vengeance Within Three Days

Dr. George B. Cressey of Shanghai College relates his recent experience with bandits on the Lwan River as follows:—

"During the past three years I have travelled many thousands of miles— Northern China, Mongolia, and Tibet—doing geological work. I have particulary been working on the problems of climatic changes in China and Eastern Asia during and since the Ice Age. This summer I originally planned to go to western Inner Mongolia for further work on the Alashan Mountains which I visited two years ago. This was out of the question with the present military situation, and so I changed to the region drained by the Lwan River in Northeastern Chihli and Jehol.

Special Pass

"Before leaving Shanghai I secured a *special* travel pass from the Consul-General, and beside the usual routine documents, the Chinese Commissioner for Foreign Affairs in Shanghai, Mr. Hsu Yuan, agreed to notify the local magistrates in Lwanchow and Jehol to extend special assistance and protection. This Shanghai pass was

here or not". In a moment, however, the tactics changed, for they began beating the crew, and in a flash overturned the straw cover in the center of the boat underneath which I was sleeping. It was dark, of course, and although I reached for my automatic, I could see nothing, all took but a second, and then I was being beaten by several sticks and in no uncertain manner ordered out of the boat.

Obeys Meekly

"Remembering account of other bandit attacks and all night forced marches, I grabbed my shoes even though the delay meant several extra blows. Some of the bandits pushed me over the side of the boat and kicked me up the muddy bank. Here Chang and I, with the three boatmen, were guarded while others of the bandits ransacked the boat. The boatmen of both boats lost their few dollars, but I was obviously the chief attraction.

"They soon found my Colt and, knowing that I must have some bullets, demanded to know where they were, putting in a couple of blows to make sure

ments, the Chinese Commissioner for Foreign Affairs in Shanghai, Mr. Hsu Yuan, agreed to notify the local magistrates in Lwanchow and Jehol to extend special assistance and protection. This Shanghai pass was issued on June 17.

"Early in July I came north via Chinwangtao, and came from there to Peking for a week of errands. I had with me a student, Mr. Chang Ping-ju, whom I left in Lwanchow with my baggage. At my instructions, he took my card to the magistrate's yamen on July 8, explained our trip, inquired whether instructions had been received from Shanghai, and left the name of the inn near the railway station where my headquarters were. This was an official call and notification to the magistrate.

No Escort

"It was stated, however, that nothing had been heard from Shanghai, and although I did not leave Lwanchow until the eleventh, nothing in the way of an escort of soldiers, warning or other advice was forthcoming. This magistrate is under Chang Tso-lin; and the entire area is also controlled by Fengtien.

"The boat we finally secured for the trip up the river to Jehol was furthermore engaged through the Fengtien official in charge of boat shipments of military supplies. Thus both the civil and military authorities were aware of my trip in detail.

"My geological work was purely scientific being neither economic nor on engineering survey. On the up river trip for the first few days, we made only a few stops and I limited my work to a reconnaissance, locating critical areas for more detailed work on the down river trip.

Rumors Heard

"Rumors of bandits reached me from time to time, as they do all over China. All were vague; no down-river boats mentioned trouble.

"On the third night out, however---the 13th our boat was suddenly attacked by a band of six *tu fei* who beat me and robbed me of all my cash---over a hundred dollars---and took or destroyed other things to the value of about a thousand dollars.

"It was about eleven o'clock, when everyone on my boat and another boat were all asleep. We were tied up to a high bank when suddenly the band of men jumped down on us, and shouted:---"A soldier has escaped and we are searching to find whether he is the chief attraction.

"They soon found my Colt and, knowing that I must have some bullets, demanded to know where they were, putting in a couple of blows to make sure that I did not hesitate to inform them. Everything I had was completely ransacked, and if cases did not open easily, they were broken with an axe. Money and guns were their chief object but plenty of other items attacted their fancy too. Unfortunately they found my flashlight and thus located a number of things which otherwise might have escaped.

"Pei Tieh"

"In all the confusion they could not find my money, and this made them even more angry, the local *tu hwa* for silver was *pei tieh*—white iron. I did not recognize what they wanted, and to each inquiry I protested ignorance and so they beat me even more severely. I finally discovered what it was they were looking for. I knew they would find it sooner or later, and so I located the box in which were 124 silver dollars and several hundred coppers. It was not a pleasant task to turn it over to them, you may be sure.

"They did not want my kodaks, but tore the case of one and broke a part of my best one. My binoculars too were not taken away, but intentionally or otherwise they smashed the lenses. My clothing was torn and trampled in the mud and when they left things were in a sorry mess. Broken eggs mixed with films, papers soaked and torn, ink and iodine on instruments, smashed cases with their original contents scattered over the muddy river bank. The bandits stayed about 45 minutes and did a thorough job.

Nervous Bandits

"While several were going through my belongings, the others guarded Chang and me and the boatmen. They were very excited and nervous, and if I made a move two or three resounding blows would descend back. Those who had a pistol brandished it in my face to frighteen me; and although they did not succeed in their purpose, it was a nervous strain to imagine whether the pistol could not accidentally go off. All of the beating was without provocation, for I did not fight back and give no resistance.

"Ths bandits were about six in number. The leader had on something of a soldier's uniform and was quite familiar with guns. The others were dressed like farmers; one or two had a queue, several had old blue clothes, and some had a handker-

1928年
鄂尔多斯与阿拉善考察计划

THE ORDOS AND THE ALASHAN

Notes on
A geological expedition to Kansu and Inner Mongolia by George B. Cressey, Ph.D., Department of Geology, Shanghai College

Time

Leave Shanghai June 5th, 1928, return September.

Route

Boat to Hankow; Peking-Hankow Railroad to Chengchow, Honan; Lung-Hai Railroad to Shanchow, Honan; Automobile to Sianfu, Shensi and Pingliang, Kansu; Pack animal to Ninghsia, Kansu. Three weeks travel from Shanghai

Return by the same route or across the central Ordos desert to Paotowchen at the end of the Peking-Suiyuan Railroad and thence to Peking.

Area

The area which it is proposed to study lies in western Inner Mongolia, north of the Great Wall from Kansu. Except for irrigated strips along the Yellow River all of this region is a desert. In the center of the area lie the great Alashan range of mountains which rise to over 10,000 feet and divide the desert into two distinct regions, the Alashan desert on the west and the Ordos on the east. The Ordos includes the district within the great northward bend of the Yellow River outside the Great Wall.

Although an ancient Mongolian trade route crosses this district, it has seldom been followed by foreigners. Except for the few trails most of the Ordos and Alashan is quite unknown, both geographically and geologically.

Marco Polo crossed the area on his journey to China, and during much of the summer the expedition will be following in his footsteps.

The Chinese city of Ninghsia and the Mongol trade center of Wangyeh fu will be the headquarters for work.

Object

The chief geological problem deals with changes in the climate of central Asia during the last few geological periods. During the Glacial Period in Europe and North America Asia was free from ice. Mongolia, furthermore, appearently had a much more moist climate. This problem is of more than theoretical interest for climate controls vegetation, and thus influences animal life. Since Asia seems to have been the center of human evolution, climate throws light on the habitability of this area. The record of climate is written in sediments and erosion cycles, and the preliminary studies made in 1924 indicate that this area contains critical information. While no direct search is to be made for ancient man, it is important to note that the best evidence of early man so far found in central Asia is on the borders of the Ordos near Ninghsia.

- 2 -

The Alashan range presents some interesting problems in structural geology, for they are formed as the result of a great thrust from the west. Similar mountains are known in other countries, but no detailed studies of this type have been made in China. It is planned to examine the general geology of the range and map its structure.

The desert is the geologists paradise. All the agents of erosion and transportation and actively at work, for despite the limited rainfall with which they carry on their work there is no protecting vegetation to anchor the soil. Geologic processes are demonstrated on every hand, often is text book perfection.

Many writers have pointed to Mongolia with its great expanses of empty land as the place to which people may emigrate from the overcrowded plains of China proper. It is hoped to study the agricultural possibilities of this area, and to estimate its economic future.

Previous Work

Both the Ordos and the Alashan were visited in 1924 on the return from an expedition to Lake Koko Nor in Tibet. There was no opportunity for detailed studies at that time, but hasty examination indicated several promising areas. Since that time the few available reports of earlier explorers have been examined and definite projects mapped out.

An attempt to continue work in 1926 resulted in an attack by brigands before the area was reached. Mongolia itself is characteristically peaceful, but the Chinese borderlands are often in an unsettled condition. Reports indicate that conditions along the route which it is not proposed to follow are quiet.

General

This is the land of wandering nomads who pasture their flocks of sheep and camels on the sparse desert grass. The rainfall is less than ten inches, and wells are few and far between. It will often be necessary to carry water. Camels are commonly used, but they travel at night and only ten miles a day; for the most part pack animals will therefore be used.

Geologically the map is white, and large areas are geographically unknown as well. Two Russian explorers, Prevelasky and Obruchef, visited the region sixty years ago and most of our knowledge dates back to them.

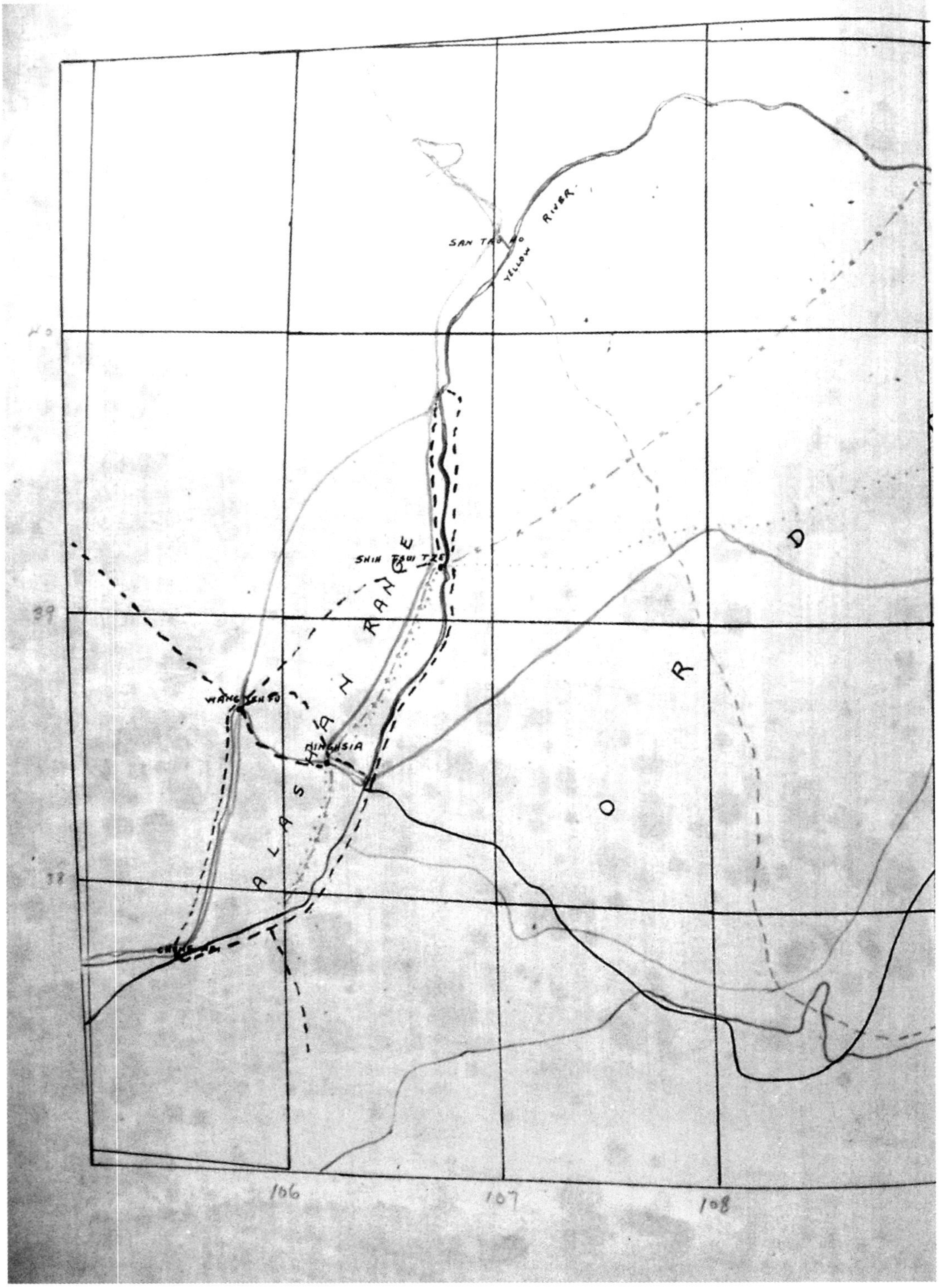
SAN TAO HO
YELLOW RIVER
SHIN TSUI TZE
WANG YEH FU
NINGHSIA
ALASHAN RANGE
ORD
40
39
38
106
107
108

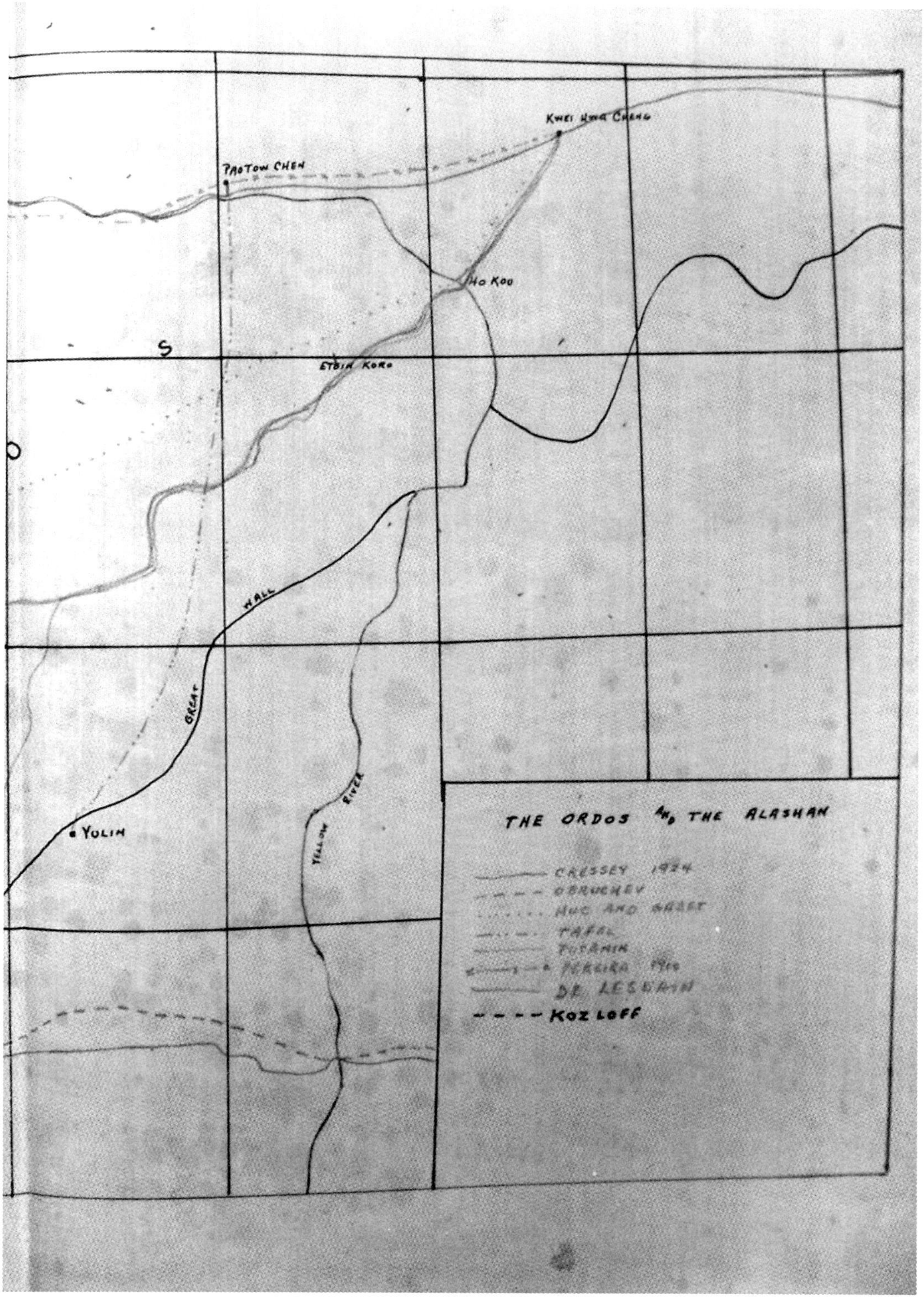
PAOTOW CHEN
HO KOU
GREAT WALL
YELLOW RIVER
YULIN
THE ORDOS AND THE ALASHAN
CRESSEY 1924
OBRUCHEV
TAFEL
PEREIRA 1910
DE LESDAIN
KOZLOFF

1928年
沪江大学地质地理系年度报告

THE DEPARTMENT OF GEOLOGY AND GEOGRAPHY

Annual Report 1928-29

The present year marks the fifth of the Department of Geology and Geography. Inasmuch as it is the last before the writer returns to America it may be well to call attention to the condition of the department. Occasional semester courses in both geology and geography have been offered for a number of years but without equipment and by various teachers. The writer came to China in 1923 via Siberia and Mongolia and spent the first yearc in language study in Peiping and in extensive travel south to Kwangtung and west to Tibet. The department was organized in the fall of 1924 and regular work has been carried on since that time.

Although no special appropriations have been available for equipment, materials have gradually been accumulated and the department is now in excellent condition. It occupies seven rooms on the fourth floor of the Science Building. The collections of rocks, minerals and fossils includes material from three continents and totals more than 5000 specimens. A small but growing museum makes some of this material available to the public. The collections of maps of China are quite complete and there are more than 800 lantern slides. The total value of the entire equipment exceeds $5000.00 The chief needs are for more geographic material, museum cases, and laboratory supplies.

Ten semester courses are now listed in the catalogue, some of them being given in alternate years. The enrollment averages 100 students.

Geology and geography occupy a unique position in the college for they are one of the few such departments in China, Yenching being the only other Christian college and Peiping and National Central in Nanking the only government schools to do serious work. The presence of such a department in a college of 600 students is an unusual thing even abroad. If it is to be continued, distinct recognition of this fact should be made. The number of students in a school of such size who might be expected to elect more than a cultural course in the Earth Sciences is naturally limited. Even such a course is impossible for many students on account of conflicts and the large number of other courses recently added to the curriculum. Geology and geography are normally of minor rank in comparison with many other subjects, so that if they are to be offered in Shanghai College at all they should be given recognized standing.

- 2 -

The department has occupied an anomolous situation with regard to the various groups of the college. Dating from the time of occasional one semester courses in general geology before the arrival of the writer, all students in the Social Science and Christian Work groups were required to take geology. This requirement was removed three years ago at the request of the writer, and all courses are now elective. At the same time the grant-in-aid of the China Medical Board for pre-medical education has greatly strengthened the work in Biology, Chemistry and Physics, and so many courses in these departments are now required that it is impossible for a student in the natural sciences to take a course in the department until the Junior year, at which time the geography courses are no longer open and the introductory course in geology normally given to Sophmores is usually closed by conflicts. The fact that the department has not shared in the financial prosperity of the other divisions of the Natural Science group and the peculiar curriculum situation has created an unfortunate lack of adjustment. Although technically in the Natural Science group very few students of that group have been able to elect work in the department and the registration has been very largely of students of other groups who are naturally are not interested in more than a course or two. The social and economic aspects of geography would easilly justify such relationships but the department has no ranking in these other groups and students receive no credit for such courses within their major group requirements. Attention has been called to this situation on several occasions.

Geology and geography deal with quite different aspects of the earth, one physical and the other human. Although there are many points of contact the two subjects have no more in common that S Sociology and Agriculture. It is thus a very difficult task for one teacher to cover the entire field. An additional instructor is an urgent need, not so much to give new courses as to make adequate preparation possible for the work now offered. Laboratory work should be a regular part of both subjects but at present is impossible.

During the past five years the department has been able to make a large contribution through research and extension. The writer has travelled more than 30,000 miles in China and has delivered over a hundred lectures, both in Shanghai and in nearby cities. The usual open lectures were given at the college in March, the subjects being "Travels in Tartary: the Ordos and the Alashan" "The Panorama of Life", "A Geographic Interpretation of Japan", and "The Sculpture of the Earth". During the summer of 1926 an expedition was undertaken to Inner Mongolia but was turned back by bandits before completing its work. During the spring of 1929 the writer is planning to attend the Fourth Pacific Science Congress in Java as a representative of the National Research Council of the United States and the Science Society of China, as well as of the college. A large part of the investigations of the year have centered around the geography of China, and the manuscript of a text book is nearly completed. These studies have been made possible by a generous grant of $3500.00 from the Institute of Pacific Relations and the Social Science Research Council.

- 3 -

In closing this report the writer would like to call the attention of the Administration and the Board of Directors to the following points.

1. Since very few institutions offer work in the Earth Sciences at all, the department occupies a unique position in the college which calls for special recognition. This is especially true on account of our small student body and many competing courses.

2. The organized status of the department with regard to the various groups is not on a satisfactory basis. This arises from the pre-medical emphasis and the social and economic nature of geography.

3. An additional instructor is urgently needed, and there should be a slight increase in the work appropriation. The writer expresses the strong hope that such a person may be secured for the coming year and that the work already started may not abandoned.

4. There should be frank and official recognition of research and extension as integral parts of the work, with provision for them within the department. It is not fair to expect such work to be carried on in addition to a full teaching load, nor for the very heavy expenses of field work to be born personally.

1928年
葛德石为发展地质地理系上校长书

August 17, 1928

Dear President Liu:

The following memorandum is in reply to your letter concerning the Five Year Policy. I am interpreting this as a statement of the scope and organization of the Department of Geology and Geography as I should like to see it in the near future.

1. Position There should be a recognition of the unique place of geology and geography in Shanghai College. Although normally minor subjects they are offered so rarely in China that if the college desires to mantain a department at all it should be willing to place it fully on a par with the other science work.

2. Staff There should be an Instructor in addition to the head. This additional person should be a returned student with special training in geography. The teaching load should be adjusted to provide time for travel, research, writing and extension.

3. Teaching The emphasis in the elementary courses should continue to be broadly cultural and inspirational. Laboratory work should be added for its training in exactness. As political conditions become more stable, the department should train students for teaching and professional positions.

4. Research There should be official recognition of the opportunity and obligation to contribute to the knowledge of the earth sciences in China. The department should have as one of its definite tasks the discovery and dissemination of information.

5. Finances There should be provision either within the budget or from special funds for travel. Both geology and geography are essentially field subjects, and it is unfair to expect necessary field work to be financed personally.

6. Equipment Our present equipment is one of the best in the country, but needs to be strengthened as regards library facilities, demonstration material, and laboratory equipment. This is particularly true for geography.

7. Relationships Despite several helpful readjustments during the past year by the Dean, the department is still imperfectly adjusted to the registration requirements of the five

- 2 -

major groups. Thus geology as a natural science is rarely elected by students of that group, although it is particularly valuable to Middle School teachers. This peculiar situation is largely due, I believe, to oub registration requirements. Likewâse geography is more of a social and economic subject yet technically it is linked with geology. In this connection I would like to suggest the advisability of reviewing our present organization.

If the foregoing items do not cover your requirements I shall be glad to supply further information.

Sincerely yours,

George B. Cressey

March 17, 1928

Dear Dr. Liu;

The following information is in response to your request of the 15th.

1. With regard to the courses to be offered next year I am unable to give this information until the question of the two appropriations from the Institute of Pacific Relations is settled. These projects have been approved by the China Council and Honolulu, and must now go to the Foundations in New York.

The courses which I should like to see the department offer if we can get the right man in geography are as follows. Courses now given are underlined, courses to be possibly omitted next year are in parentheses.

	Geography	Geology
Freshman	101 World Activities	--
	102 Geographic Influences	--
Sophomore	--	101 Physical
	--	102 Historical
Junior	103 China	103 (Petrology)
	104 Rest of Asia	104 (Economic)
Senior	105-106 Subject undetermined	105-106 Principles

2. Research projects recently completed are as follows:

The Climate of Eastern Asia during the Glacial Period.
The Geology of Shanghai.
The Geography of China.

Research projects still in progress:

Glaciation in Asia during the Pleistocene.
The habitability of central Asia during the time of man's evolution.
The origin and climatic meaning of the loess
sub-project The loess of the Nanking Hills.
Other geologic and geographic problems in Manchuria and Mongolia.

- 2 -

Research projects proposed for next year:

Field studies in the Ordos and Alashan deserts of Inner Mongolia during June, July and August, dealing with desert processes, climatic changes, geographic influences, and agricultural possibilities.

The preparation of a new base map of China, compiled de novo from original sources. This will form the base for about two dozen maps dealing with climate, topography, agriculture, population and human use. To be published as an atlas of Comparative Geography by the Commercial Press.

Completion of a book on the geography of China, involving studies of natural resources, conditions of life, and regional geography. In cooperation with the Institute of Pacific Relations.

Cooperation with the University of Nanking in an extensive field investigation of Land Utilization.

3.

The extension service of the department consists of lectures both on the campus and elsewhere. More than twenty will be given during the present year. It is proposed to continue this next year. As much writing will be done as secretarial assistance may make possible.

4.

Requested budget for the coming year.

Present appropriation This includes heat, light, janitor service and upkeep, as well as scientific equipment, operating expenses and travel for visiting speakers.	$ 650.00
Instructor Returned student at $150, per month The Institute of Pacific Relations will probably pay the college $1320, so that the college will need to add $480. This person will teach part time and do research under my direction.	1800.00
Total budget requested	$ 2450.00

Sincerely yours,

George B. Cressey

第二章（1934）

1928 年，国民政府定都南京使江浙两省成为国家政权统治的核心地带，因而也是政府锐意经营的“模范省区”。在国民党人引以为自豪的“十年建设”时期（1927—1937），江浙两省的建设事业确实都取得不小的成就。1934 年 7 月，前来中国研究的葛德石被南京国民政府任命为江浙两省特别地理协调员。7 月 26 日，葛德石从南京至上海，8 月 1 日到达杭州。他通过汽车、轿子、小船、步行等方式，先后考察了金华、丽水、温州、宁波、新昌、长兴、江山、瞿州、严州等地，至 8 月底结束考察，行程近五千公里，调查内容主要包括地形、土壤、气候特征和农作物等。本部分收录整理了这一年葛德石的考察计划。

1934年
中国考察计划

Geographic Field Work in China

George B. Cressey

A This survey is designed to throw light on geographic conditions within several small selected areas in China. Each study will involve two to three weeks of residence, spent mostly in detailed mapping, and will result in a comprehensive picture of the physical and cultural landscape in these areas.

The work is a continuation of field studies carried on from 1923 to 1929 and research in this country since that time. The broader regional aspects of this program have just appeared in book from under the title of CHINA'S GEOGRAPHIC FOUNDATIONS. It is now proposed to critically examine the more detailed adjustments of human activities within typical localities, chosen with reference to their regional relations. The number of studies will be governed by the available time, probably four to six.

Problems of land use underly many aspects of China's difficulties. By means of geographic analysis of individual communities it is hoped to provide a more adequate appreciation of present realities and future potentialities. The work will involve a study of topographic adjustments, climatic and soil factors, patterns of occupance, economic activities, and the historical background.

Cressey - 2

Field work will be carried on in close cooperation with the China Land Utilization Survey which is under the direction of Dr. J. Lossing Buck of the University of Nanking, supported by the Institute of Pacific Relations. The program was first outlined in 1939 while the writer was still in China, and has been in contemplation for this stage of the Survey since that time. During the interval the Survey has collected statistical data on agriculture and economic conditions in over 100 type areas, while the writer has completed his volume on geographic regions.

The proposed project is designed to provide a geographic background and evaluation of the data shortly to be published by the Survey, and at the same time will greatly benefit from the information and field assistance to be provided by Professor Buck's group. One or more of Professor Buck's men will be with the writer throughout the summer.

The areas selected for field work are, tentatively, in the Canton-Hongkong region, the Yangtze delta, the Red Basin of Szechwan, and between Peiping and Tientsin. Except for Szechwan each of these districts have been visited by the writer and all published maps and data have been assembled. One or two studies may be in areas not covered by the Land Utilization Survey

Cressey - 3

In some districts attention will be focused on the principal crop or occupation, in another study communications may be emphasized, and elsewhere a market village and its tributary area will be examined. Actual details must await arrival, but the common objective is to understand the adjustments between man and nature. In each area I plan to stay in native inns or if practical with a missionary family. While I do not need an interpretor, I may have a Chinese student as an assistant.

Geographic studies in China are almost non-existant, and very few American geographers have research interests in this part of the world. The writer's qualifications include a conversational familiarity with Chinese, experience in interior travel, and the background represented in the completion of CHINA'S GEOGRAPHIC FOUNDATIONS. This volume is an outgrowth of Social Science Research Council grants in 1929 and 1932, and constitutes the principal exhibit in support of the present application.

Cressey - 4

B Similar studies are well known in this country and in Japan, but are unavailable for China. The proposed project differs from much of the writer's previous work in that reconaissance necessarilly preceeds detailed investigation. The two fit into a logical sequence and are part of a long-time plan.

C The background of the project is to be found in my six years of travel and research in China (1923-29), culminating in CHINA'S GEOGRAPHIC FOUNDATIONS (1934).

In preparation for the work of next summer I have spent nearly $100. for maps, have prepared travel plans, and am developing possible techniques. The fund of information gathered by the China Land Utilization Survey makes it possible to work with unusual efficiency.

D The project is essentially dependent upon assistance from the Social Science Research Council and the National Research Council. The desired grants will cover field expenses from May to October, 1934.

E Office work in Syracuse will require perhaps a year preparatory to publication.

F Some of the material will be included in the final reports of the China Land Utilization Survey, but most of the studies will presumably appear as separate journal articles.

第三章（1943—1944）

1937 年抗战爆发以来，中国在远东战区牵制日军主力，同时付出巨大代价。为了改善中国未被占领地区的生活条件，提高教育水平和鼓舞中国的士气，1942 年美国国务院启动中美文化外交项目（Cultural Relations Program）。从 1942—1945 年间，美国前后共派出 30 名农业、工业、新闻以及医学等领域的专家赴华，在战时中国发挥了积极作用。1943 年 11 月至 1944 年 6 月，葛德石作为美国国务院访问教授来华。在华期间，葛德石走访大学、研究机构，举行演讲，输送资料。本部分收录整理了葛德石该期间在中国考察的有关报告和档案、文献。

葛德石在战时中国的考察，包括在西南中国，特别是对大学的考察与评估，是我们了解抗战时期中国高等教育的重要史料。而葛德石的《告中国人民书》，反映了作为地理学家的葛德石对中美关系的理解。

1943年
地缘策略演讲稿

Geopolitics in the Air Age

(Geostrategy)

a talk prepared for delivery before the Chinese-American Institute of Cultural Relations, Chungking, Dec. 22, 1943, by George B. Cressey

- Sino Am Cult Inst.
- Natl. Central Univ.

Kunming Rotary

Lien ta

We live in a new world, a round world, a small world; we live in one world. Whoever wins this war, and we are determined to achieve unconditional victory, one thing is certain about the second half of the Twentieth Century. No longer will Europe and America live in an Atlantic hemisphere with little concern about the other half. The world of tomorrow will be all the world without an east or west.

We have learned that today there are no wars but world wars, and there are no wars but total wars. We must also learn that there is no peace but world peace, and no peace but total peace. We did not recognize that an incident on Sept. 18, 1931 would engulf the world, but it is now clear that the Society of Nations must collectively watch trouble wherever it starts. The world cannot live half peaceful and half chaotic, nor half rich and half poor.

The problems which we face are many, and geography can contribute only a part of the answer, but it does provide an essential foundation and framework. What kind of a planet is this on which we live? Our modern material society places great emphasis on raw materials: on iron ore and coal, on oil and water power, on copper and aluminum, and on a host of equally important commodities.

When the United States was cut off from access to the tin and manganese and chromium of Southeastern Asia, and to its rubber and quinine and cocoanut oil and manila hemp, we suddenly realized our industrial dependance on such ~~commodities.~~ products No less important than minerals ~~is are~~ good soil and suitable climate and favorable topography and strategic location. These desirable gifts of nature are not evenly distributed.

Siberia differs from India, and Chungking from Tihwa. Nature seems to have played favorites for the good things of the world are very unevenly ~~distributed~~ located. The first lesson of geography is thus interdependance. If we wish to live a full life, at least in the Twentieth Century material sense, we must supply our wants from distant sources. No nation or even continent can be self sufficient. Trade and interdependance are inescapable.

The unity and inter~~dependance~~relationship of this new world means that we must rethink our geography. We must recognize the global aspect of all problems, whether economic , social or political. In the beginings of history, man's travels were limited to the land and rivers and smaller lakes. Then civilization spread to the enclosed seas to the Mediterranean in the Occident and to the East China Sea in the Orient. From the great land mass of Eurasia and these intermediate water bodies, settlement reached the new world of the Americas. Whereas oceans were once barriers which separated the lands, they are now highways which link all the earth. Across them flow people, goods, and ideas. We have sometimes regretted that Columbus and Balboa discovered the last continent and the last ocean, leaving no more exploration for us. Yet within our lifetime has occurred the greatest geographic discovery of ~~all~~ history. Before our eyes is opened the largest area of all, a world-wide ocean, the ocean of the air. Our generation is to be the greatest race of geographic pioneers in all history.

The world has not been flat since the days of Magellan, but our maps are still drawn on flat pieces of paper. Thus we fail to understand the roundness of the world. Only a globe can be honest, for the earth is a sphere and the paper necesarilly flat. Every flat map is thus somewhat dishonest, unless we read it correctly. One of the major requirements for world citizenship is a global understanding of our problems, whether of transportation, food, or government.

Airplanes can fly anywhere. They hurdle mountains and deserts and easily cross every ocean. Instead of winding through valleys and avoiding swamplands, the highways of the air follow direct great circle routes. Places that were once remote are now near. The old maps always showed continental boundaries because these were transition zones where one changed from boats to wheeled vehicles. They also gave political boundaries for there the traveller must go through customs and immigration formalities. The new maps of the air need not show land and sea, but only places. One of the most striking recent advertisements in the American press was a full page map of the northern hemisphere on a polar projection, which gave only place names served by airplanes, without any continental outlines. These new air age maps look different. One of the major problems of the Peace Conference will be to define the new freedom of the air, just as we have long had the freedom of the seas.

Do you know how far it is from North America to Europe?; less than 400 minutes by air, in fact some planes have flown across the Atlantic in six hours. It may be thousands of miles by sea, or a week by steamer, but it is less than 400 minutes by air, - and a fraction of a second by radio.

Do you know how far it is from Chungking to Kunming? It may be five hundred miles by road which means several uncomfortable days by truck, but it is only three hours by air. How this has changed, and how different our maps would appear if we used a scale of hours instead of a scale of miles. May I give you an example. Travel in Yunnan was once limited to sedan chairs and was made hazardous by banditry. Only fifteen years ago a missionary family, transferred from northeastern Yunnan to southwestern Yunnan, found it cheaper, much safer, and actually quicker to travel by way of Chungking, Shanghai, Singapore and Rangoon, rather than to go overland with porters.

From Chungking to Tokyo may be several years for victory, but the 2000 air line miles can easily be covered in daylight.

We need not only to relearn our time scale, but our compass as well. Which way is New York City from Chungking? Ordinarilly we would travel eastward, although I had to come from the west, but the shortest course is due north directly over the pole. Did you know that the great circle course from Seattle to Tokyo passes north of the Aleutian Islands?, or that the great circle route from Panama to Manila goes north of the Hawaiian Islands and very close to Tokyo?

Supply problems of refueling may postpone trans-Arctic flying, but the route via Alaska is only slightly longer. Mrs. Lindberg chose an appropriate title for her book when she wrote "North to the Orient"

The post war world will have a new geography. When we in China formerly went to Europe, we travelled via Shanghai and Singapore, or perhaps by way of Vancouver and Canada. Tomorrow we will go by rail to Rangoon, and thence by ship. And day after tomorrow we will go all the way by rail via Sinkiang. The direct air route from Chungking to London,xxxxxx only 4000 miles or an easy day's flight, passes directly through Tihwa and Moscow.

In this air world no place on the planet is more than 60 hours flying time from anywhere else. From Chungking you can be in the Argentine in $2\frac{1}{2}$ days. All this will cost something, and we cannot all afford to fly around the world, but some people will, and mail will, and so will ideas.xxxxx

This is one world, and a small one There is no geography but global geography, and no aspect of human life but what affects all others. As citizens of the new world, our required assignment is to think not only of our own country and hemisphere, but of the globe as a whole. And may I again remind you that the first lesson of geography is interdependance.

All of this may seem an overlengthy preface to geopolitics,

5

but as the world is one, so geography is all one. For academic purposes we sometimes divide geography into its economic or political or cultural phases. This convenient and proper, but today everything has ~~a~~ political implications. The American Secretary of State, Mr. Cordell Hull, has repeatedly sought to improve world trade conditions as a necessary prerequisite to international peace. Cultural intercourse also leads to political understanding. The considerable measure of good will which links China and the United States arises from the interchange of Chinese students who have come to our country and the American missionaries who have come to yours.

Political geography is no magic formula or subtle implement of national policy, nor can it be separated from other aspects of geographic concern. Nor likewise can geography be isolated from the whole of life and environment. Since geography is so new, as well as so old, it may be well to comment on its scope and objectives. Its task is ~~merely~~ to study places, to ~~study~~ examine the significance of areas and locations and all the interrelated things which go on there. Some of these characteristics of place and area concern government, others relate to livlihood or culture, but all are part of the whole.

Geographers have always been concerned with boundaries and colonies and trade barriers. Thus political geography is an old and recognized field, but one which has dealt for the most part with describing situations rather than with designing means for implementing policy. The sudden popular interest in the subject is because the Germans have perverted it into a dynamic tool for imperialistic goals under the term of geopolitics. Within the past two or three years there have been a dozen volumes on geopolitics in English, and every American magazine finds it fashionable to carry an article on its German leader, Karl Haushofer. It is perhaps significant that this literature, for the most part, is not written by geographers or political scientists but by ~~German~~ European refugees.

Position is important equally in peace and war, for it involves not only physical location but also accessibility and the geographic qualities which make some places more desirable than others. These are active factors, and as such bring consequences, planned or otherwise. The word strategy deals with the application of policy, and calls for a recognition of the significance of place and all that goes with it. This covers more than merely political geography, so that the comon term of geopolitics seems adequate; instead it appears better to coin the new word geostrategy for all those dynamic aspects of applied international geography. It may thus include all the geographic factors of trade, production, and intercourse which bear upon world problems.

An understanding of geopolitics, or geostrategy, is not in itself a solution for international problems, but it is clear that geographic ignorance is immeasurably expensive. When the United States acquired the Philippine Islands from Spain fifty years ago, the American delegates to the peace conference did not have a ~~proper~~ adequate map of what they were buying. They thus failed to include the Sulu Archipelago which was properly a part of the Philippines, hence a subsequent conference and payment of $50,000 was necessary; indeed two other treaties were necessary before the full extent of the islands were defined. At that time the now-Japanese mandated islands also belonged to Spain and could have been acquired by the United States if our statesmen had had adequate foresight. Instead Spain some years later sold them to Germany, from whom they were transferred to Japan after the First World War. And it was from these islands that Japan attacked Pearl Harbor, and it is Japan's posession of these islands which prevents a frontal attack on Japan today.

7

The vast spaces of Asia have been a favorite field for writers in geopolitics. Unfortunately many of them have too little understood the geography of the continent which they have tried to explain, and have equally failed to think adequately in terms of a round world. Almost none of the geopoliticians have considered the meaning of the air age.

German theories of geopolitics visualize the state as an organism, and as such in need of living room; only as it grows and expands can it live. Thus aggression and war are essential to survival. Under Herr General Professor Karl Haushofer at Munich, there developed the Institut fur Geopolitik. This brought together a large group of geographers and others who studied the economic and political geography of the world in detail. Out of these elaborate studies the Institute formulated dynamic plans for action by means of which Germany might achieve her place in the sun. Haushofer gave relatively little attention to the New World as any advance westward toward France and Britain appeared too difficult. Instead the natural line of expansion was thought to lie in the East, toward and into the Soviet Union and incidentally south to Africa. Many of these ideas are echoed in Adolf Hitler's "Mein Kampf." Thus under Haushofer's direction, political geography, under the guise of "geopolitik", was perverted into a tool for imperialism.

Behind the plans of Haushofer lies a significant volume by a great British geographer, Sir Halford Mackinder, entitled "Democratic Ideals and Reality" This was written at the close of the First World War as a warning to the Allied peacemakers that peace could only be ensured by securely enclosing Germany on the east, preferably by a corridor of buffer states between Germany and Russia. Mackinder viewed history as a contest between land power and sea power. The latter can outflank land power, and draw on distant supplies through command of the ocean, but it needs an adequate home base. Land power can win in the long run if it has

8

It was this idea which lead Haushofer to many of his conclusions

resources, size, and location. '

Mackinder contended that Europe, Asia and Africa formed a "World Island" which dominated the world. Within interior Asia he described a mountain-and desert-enclosed "Heartland" which in turn was the key to the security of the World Island. Since this core was remote from the ocean and inaccessible to naval power, it was an invulnerable fortress. Only on the west, next to Europe, was it approachable, and only through European technique and capital could it be developed. Hence his famous statement: "Who rules eastern Europe commands the Heartland; who rules the Heartland commands the World Island, Who rules the World Island commands the World" It was to prevent German access to the gates of the Heartland that Mackinder advocated the creation of the corridor states of Poland, Czechoslovakia, and so on.

This Asiatic Heartland includes all of the Soviet Union except the part drained by the Pacific and that west of the Volga. It also took in Mongolia, Tibet, Sinkiang, and Iran. This area is large, and on the whole well supplied with mineral resources, but the agricultural possibilities are poor, and the population is never likely to be numerous in comparison with the rest of the world. It has size, but it would appear to lack the essentials of political strength. A castle is not strong merely because it is large.

At least ten factors are significant in geostrategy, whether in war or in peace. Few areas have all, but a country or region which is deficient in many of them can scarcely expect to achieve international greatness. These elements of geostrategy are 1. size 2. shape, 3. accessibility, 4 location, 5. boundaries, 6. relation to the ocean, 7. land forms, 8 minerals, 9 climate, and perhaps most important of all 10 people. May I now procedd to analise each of the ten.

The impostance of size was dramatically demonstrated during the earlier years of the Second World War. One of a nation's greatest military assets today is defense in depth. Thus both the Soviet Union and China were able to retreat before the enemy and thereby gain time for further resistance; to sell space in order to buy time. In contrast to these large countries, Belgium and even Poland lacked adequate size and so were wiped out in a week. But mere size is not enough. No large army could retreat into Mongolia or Tibet or northern Siberia and survive, for there are inadequate productive facilities. Too great an area may be a handicap unless well developed and united. The Heartland of Mackinder is large and remote, but it is devoid of the possibilities for major economic strength.

Now that wars are three-dimensional, there are no longer any buffer states nor any front. No existing country anywhere is large enough to be immune from air attack, or to furnish an adequate base for world conquest. In the next war there will be no secure places, even in the largest countries. Mackinder overlooked the fact that his Heartland is just over the top of the world from North America. The new air age has upset all considerations of land power versus sea power.

Form or shape is the second element is geostrategy. A nation like Chile is so drawn out that while her area equals that of Germany, economic unity is made difficult. Canada appears compact on the map, but her population is as attenuated as that of Chile, no more than a fringe along the boundary of the United States. While Mackinder's Heartland has a satisfactory gross shape, the distribution of good land and minerals and communications within it is so eccentric that the form lacks coherence.

Accessibility is of major importance in political geography. Anything more than mere subsistance requires trade and communications. One of the major problems of China today is that of adequate access to the outside world, and one of the most conspicuous developments in the post war years will doubtless be the great improvement in internal communications. Within Asia today, no road links India with the Soviet Union and but one highway leads from India to China. Unfortunately there is not even a road from India to Burma. Northern Siberia has only its rivers, ice-bound for much of the year. Vast areas of interior Asia today are entirely out of reach of railways, navigable rivers or even poor automobile roads. With such a condition, modern participation in a world society is almost impossible. Accessibility is thus one of the key factors in the geographic aspect of of human relations.

4 The fourth element is location. This is the prime question in all of geography, not "where" in terms of latitude and longitude, but "where" in terms of good land and markets and world highways. Shanghai does not owe its importance to its latitude but to the hinterland of the Yangtze valley. The mouths of the great Siberian rivers lack good harbors, but the productivity of the interior is forcing port developments. Throughout history the Russian Bear has sought warm water, an outlet to the unfrozen ocean. Position is inescapably important in political policy and economic orientation.

The Heartland represents the climax of continentality, but few nations have achieved cultural progress or national greatness without external contacts. China may have wished that she did not have such an exposed coast line, but the peacetime assets greatly outweigh the military liabilities. Japan enjoys an excellent position in the western Pacific but she lacks a secure home base. Her defeat today has become so difficult because of her ~~secure~~ interior position within her newly enlarged empire, and the difficulty of getting at the central core.

The significance of location can change. Thus Rome was once the center of the civilized world, but the Mediterranean is now a minor body of water. Central Asia is increasing its population, but there is no liklihood that it will ever hold the controlling party of mankind, or that the Mongols will ever again rule half the continent.

5 Boundaries frequently present problems; here is the fifth component of geostrategy. Sir Halford Mackinder followed deserts and

mountains in defining his Heartland citadal. These form natural obstacles to ground travel, but do not stop airplanes. If such barriers keep armies from trespassing, they equally keep out trade and ideas. No civilization can progress without stimulating contacts. Thus while China hasx empty frontiers along much of the interior, she is open to world ideas in the east.

6 The ocean is still the cheapest highway, and will continue to be of great importance in the air age. Without free access to it a nation suffers. One might even trace history in terms of progressively larger and larger water bodies, from the Nile to the Aegean and Mediterranean and Atlantic, and in some measure in the future to the Pacific. Oceans are highways not barriers.

7. Topography is the seventh element. Here Asia suffers, for rugged ranges isolate its various realms. The Himalayas assuredly provide the Heartland with security from invasion on the south, but they also block trade. China has benifited during the Japanese invasion by having such poor roads in her hill country, but if there had been better roads for a decade previously China might have been strong enough to resist effectively.

8. Raw materials, both mineral and agricultural, are vital in our modern world. Other nations in other times have achieved conspicuous success in art or philosophy, but in the Twentieth Century national greatness rests, perhaps too much, upon coal, oil, iron, copper, and aluminum. Lord Curzon once remarked that during the First World War, the Allies "floated to victory on a sea of oil". Thus during the Second World War they are flying to victory on a cloud of gasolene. To fly five tons of freight from America to China takes something like fifty tons of gasolene. These natural resources are distributed very unevenly. The Soviet Union is exceptionally rich, second only to the United States. India has great deposits of iron ore but very inadequate coal with which to smelt it. Japan showed great resourcefullness in developing her varied resources, but

their ammounts are limited. China is the richest nation around the western Pacific, but her per capita reserves are modest except in coal. It appears probable that China has enough mineral wealth to provide for spectacular industrialization in a few limited areas for some decades, but it is not likely that China will become a manufacturing area comparable to western Europe or the eastern United States.

Climate is often overlooked as a national resource, yet health and human progress are directly related to it. It is not likely that a League of Nations will ever have its capital in the Amazon valley or Yakutsk. Nor will exceptionally energetic people ever live in these areas. Agriculture is as vitally affected as man.

The tenth and most important of this long list are people. Without them no other items have meaning, and with superior technological skill or patriotism many physical handicaps can be overcome. No mere deterministic forcast of relative impprtance of areas is possible. Traditions of self sacrifice, democratic education, or a religion dedicated to service are of inescapable geographic significance. Considerations of geostrategy must consider how many people live where, what their standards of living and abilities may be, and what their urge to world conquest. Thus man power is one of China's great assets, and the long range strength of China versus Japan is clear.

All of this adds up to saying that the geostrategy of international relations involves all of life and its environment. Where there were once once physical factors of security and isolation, today's unified world makes interdependance inescapable. Isolationism cannot even be a debatable question. If we fight, the whole world must fight, if we want peace, the whole world must have peace.

How then can a nation be sedure, what is the safest course for a country to follow? The ten elements of geostrategy have been operative for centuries, and will continue to be significant, but they will have different meaning. When and if we try to remake the political map of certain parts of the world, factors such as these must surely be considered. But no longer can any combination of them offer freedom from fear, of freedom from want, or any of the securities which we seek. If this is indeed one world, we must live together, and that means cooperation. I know of only three political avenues to peace. One is to have a single nation overwhelmingly strong, as with the Holy Roman Empire; There is no prospect of this again. Another is through a balance of power, often tried and as often leading to war. The third is collective security through an association of nations. This is the most difficult, for it is the most democratic, and it too failed the first time when tried. Cooperation must rest on good will, and that requires conscious willingness to understand the problems of other people and nations. To such an understanding, geography may make a significent contribution.

The greatness of a nation, and its secure strength, rests upon the quality of its people; their standards of living, their intelligence and adjustability, and their loyal patriotism. The demands of this war have called for unexpected skills and resourcefullness, for which noone could have specifically prepared. Should we have another war, it too may be very different and again call for adjustability. It is the unique characteristic of democratic countries that free people have these essential loyalties and skills. Here is a nation's greatest strength.

May I add one final idea. If interdependance is a sound lesson of geography; autarchy is unsound. It is of course proper for each nation to produce certain essentials, but any attempt to achieve artificial self sufficiency is certain to prove disastrous. Shortly before the outbreak of the European War, when Germany was endeavoring to develop an ersatz economy of autarchy, Mr. Hitler made a significant speech in which he said "Germany must export or perish". What he really meant was that Germany must import or perish, and that to pay for these vital imports she must find an export market. German chemists and technicians are among the most able in the world, but they found foreign trade essential. So it must be with every modern state. The first lesson of geography is interdependance. ¶ This same problem faces the United States in its opposite form. We in America have great resources and a productive capacity almost equal tothat of all the rest of the world combined. After the war we shall be eagerly looking for overseas markets. Sometime I should like to write an article under the title of "America must import or perish", for unless we are willing to buy from abroad, our would-be customers cannot pay for our products. The only bal/ance of trade which is favorable is one which balances; sooner or later imports must xxxxxxx equal exports.

Political geography, or what I have called geostrategy, is merely the background af for international relations. Under German direction it was perverted into an imperialistic tool to arouse public opinion in support of an imperialistic policy. In that sense each nation has its own gx particular brand of geopolitics. But as we move into the more global world of the air age, we should do well to rethink our place in world society. We who believe in democracy, we who believe that peoples are more important than governments, must recognize that these problems require education, and conscious devotion.

Our nations are now engaged in a great war. What is the victory which we seek? Will it come when the armies of the United Nations march down the streets of Berlin and Tokyo, will that guarentee peace and the end of our troubles? On the contrary, when the fighting stops our problems will increase. In some wars the war is won when the enemy's country is captured, but now we are fighting to create a future rather than to defend a past. To attain victory we must attain not merely military objectives but moral objectives as well.

Between the Axis Powers and the United Nations there is a basic difference in political theory, if you please in geopolitics, both external + internal. In the words of President Roosevelt, our enemies must "abandon the philosophy and the teaching of that philosophy which has brought so much suffering to the world". It will not be enough to disarm Germany as we did in 1918, we must change their world ambition and concept of the state. The war will not be won until we have eliminated the causes which made it. Our ideas must triumph over theirs, and this can be possible only if we are more devoted to them and make them more credible than theirs.

We believe in the rights of humanity, in the dignity of free men. We seek not to crush our enemies, but we are determined to eliminate from the world those fascist ideas which place the state above the citizen. Again as President Rosevelt has said "The issue of this war is the basic issue between those who believe in mankind and those who do not - the ancient issue between those who put their faith in the people and those who put their faith in dictators and tyrants" This <u>is</u> the issue. What is at stake is a great prinviple, not merely victory on the battlefield but victory for the idea that people can govern themselves, and of right should.

1943—1944年
中国高等教育考察报告

Memorandum from George B. Cressey
Cultural Relations Program, Chungking

Dec. 31, 1943

SUBJECT National Central University

ABSTRACT National Central is the second ranking university, but its plant is very inadequate and scholarship standards are declining due to inflation.

SUGGESTED DISTRIBUTION Embassy, RC, FE, American accrediting organizations

Memorandum

The National Central University is commonly regarded as the second best Chinese university, ranking next to Kunming. It is located at Shapingpa, some ten miles north of Chungking, where it moved from Nanking in 1937. I visited the campus from Dec. 27 to 30, inclusive, and have also been there on two previous occasions.

The university has had internal and political difficulties which resulted in the Generalissimo assuming the presidency some months ago. The Vice-President and acting head is Chu Ching-nung, or King Chu, who was a colleague of mine at the University of Shanghai fifteen years ago.

The campus is on a slightly hill overlooking the Chialing River. There are perhaps fifty one-story buildings, mostly of bamboo frame construction and very temporary. Some floors are wooden but most are of tamped earth. The whole plant is in bad condition and quite inadequate. For example, the blackboards are barely usable.

Guest rooms will shortly be available in the new student center, sponsored by the Y.M.C.A. under a pleasant Britisher, David Paton. I had said in advance that I appreciated the current financial conditions and did not wish them to go to special trouble, accordingly I lived the life of an ordinary professor. This meant that I was housed in a room in the professors' dormitory, currently vacant as its occupant was just recovering from typhus!, and ate in an open air mat shed restaurant where I am sure the dishes never see soap. Some of my friends were thoughtful, but on the whole I was poorly cared for and the whole impression was unfavorable. A week of chilly weather without once being in a heated room is not too comfortable. The sanitation is vile.

National Central now has 4223 students, twice the Nanking enrollment. There are seven colleges and 45 departments. One-third the total registration is in the College of Engineering, about 15per cent of the students are girls. Seventeen departments

国立中央大学备忘录（1943）

-2-

are authorized to confer the masters degree, but there is no work for the doctorate. The graduate group numbers between thirty and forty.

I made no detailed study of standards, but it is obvious and freely admitted that the quality of work has deteriorated greatly in recent years. Few textbooks are available at any price, and there is little use of mimeographed outlines etc. Students depend almost entirely upon their lecture notes. Library assigned readings are impractical. Some dormitories are without electric lights, and throughout the campus they are turned off one night a week. The usual student schedule is 20 to 22 hours a week, overcrowded due to excessive and often impractical course requirements laid out by the Ministry of Education.

All of the library was brought from Nanking, but there is shelf space for only 20 per cent of the books so that the others are stored in boxes in another building. The reading room seats perhaps 200, and was half filled when I visited it. Reference collections are by now badly worn, and almost everything which I saw could be junked after the war. Two microfilm readers are in a small room, together with three cases of shelves of microfilm. It is planned to move the material to a larger room, and to change the present wall projectors to vertical types in order to facilitate copying . Reports varied as to the usefulness of microfilm. Some said it was much used and appreciated, and that it was proposed to translate and mimeograph articles; others commented on the poor definition, eyestrain, necessity of signing up in advance, and the lack of use except by a few advanced workers. I met no one who said that they regularly went through the journals in their own field as received.

Inflation is a serious problem, and the bulk of the students and faculty are living in poverty. Faculty salaries have twice been doubled, most recently in October. Thus a teacher who received CNC $600 in Nanking now gets $2400. In addition they receive rice to the value of about $1000, and many receive "research" grants. Since it costs $8000 merely to keep a small family alive, the problem is acute. Many wives are working, and some teachers have duplicate jobs elsewhere under other names. Many have had to sell their libraries and equipment.

Teaching loads are very light, nine hours for most of the faculty and 6 hours for departmental chairmen. This is supposed to give face by emulating Harvard standards, I was told, but I see very little research or creative scholarship under way. One department chairman said to me "Why should we teach more if the government does not pay us enough to meet our expenses?"

Students are supplied with free tuition, room, and board, but have minor expenses. The poorest must spend $500 a month, while the wealthy may use $2000. The latter would thus prefer to come to America where at 20 to 1 they could easily finance themselves.

-3-

While on the campus during this and previous visits, I gave three public lectures: The Geography of Asia (distribution of agricultural land and minerals), Geopolitics in the Air Age (global relations and peace), and How to Defeat Japan (geographical aspects of attack from different directions). These were each attended by several hundred students, who seemed to understand my English without trouble. I also gave several professional talks before the geography group, and likewise in geology. I also spoke to the English Club on American university life. My remaining time was constantly occupied by conferences with faculty members who were pathetically eager for overseas news in their field.

Memorandum from George B. Cressey
Cultural Relations Program, Chungking

February 10, 1944

SUBJECT National Southwest Associated University

ABSTRACT This university, in Kunming, is usually regarded as the best in China. It has a good faculty but poor quarters and serious financial problems.

SOURCE OF DATA The writer spent three weeks in Kunming in January 1944, and gave nine lectures at the university. There were numerous apportunities for personal conference.

SUGGESTED DISTRIBUTION Embassy, FE, RC, American accrediting organizations

MEMORANDUM

Organization The National Associated Southwestern University is commonly known in Chinese as Lien ta, and is said to be the best university in the country. It is a war-time federation of Peiping National University from Peiping, the American Boxer institution known as Tsinghua University also from Peiping, and Nankai University from Tientsin. All of these were removed to Kunming after the outbreak of the war.

The University functions as a unit so far as students and courses are concerned, but each of the institutions maintains its legal identity and president. These presidents are Dr. Y. C. Mei of Tsinghua and chairman of the executive council, Dr. Chiang Mon-lin of Peiping, and Dr. Chang Polin of Nankai who spends most of his time near Chungking. Faculty contacts are commonly in the name of the professors original institution. Although this school, like most others, is under the direction of the Ministry of Education, the control is less than elsewhere.

Equipment The campus lies just outside the city wall, and is a collection of simple but orderly mud buildings. These were built with the expectation of merely a year or two's stay. The equipment is very meager, but ingenious improvisations have [illegible] made up for many deficiencies. The more valuable apparatus is kept in the country nearby for safety in air raids. Thus only enough physics apparatus is on hand for the current experiments. Fifty gallon oil drums with hinged lids are sunk into the floor of many buildings in order to provide moderate safety for irreplaceable items.

The library is very limited. Peiping was unable to bring any of its books, and a part of those brought by Tsinghua were bombed enroute. The stacks contained but 15 volumes in English on geology, with no more on reserve. Two-thirds of these were old elementary pirated editions, with bindings in tatters. Additional geology volumes were in a nearby country research center. Textbooks are almost unobtainable for most students, both due to expense and paper shortages. Mimeographed material is seldom used due to the high cost of stencils.

The reading room is large and well utilized.

西南联合大学备忘录（1944）

Cressey Memo on Southwest University 2 Feb. 10

Students The student body numbers 2500, of whom ten percent ar
Dormitories are excessively crowded, with double deck bunks and
aisle space between. Forty students live in each mud hut.
in Kunming are higher than elsewhere, and despite government s
the minimum student costs amount to $800 CNC per month. Many
spend over $2000 CNC. Since this equals US $100 at the offici
study in America a pears very attractive. Many students are se
undernourished.

Students prefer to remain at Lien ta because of the supe
educational standards and faculty, despite the greater costs. Th
also a faint hope that after the war when the universities return t
their former location, student travelling expenses may also be care

Many of the seniors have already left, and the current gra
will do likewise, in order to join the Chinese Army as interpreters c
other assistants to the American forces in China.

Faculty The high rank of Lien ta is determined by its faculty, many of whom are genuine scholars. Out of a total staff of some 400, over 180 hold American advanced degrees. The group is undoubtedly the strongest nucleus of western civilization in China, and deserves support

Salaries have been increased about ten fold, but the cost of living is up fully 400 times. The maximum salaries with rice allowances are now $5500 CNC, more often $4000 CNC. The faculty are shortly to receive supplements back to October of $1300 CNC a month. I visited several faculty homes, of people of some professional distinction, and found serious poverty and acute need, though perhaps not actual distress. Many teachers have secured part time employment, especially in connection with the local American Army program. Since teaching loads are very light, supposedly to promote research, some of the faculty are able to devote two-thirds of their time to outside work.

Clerks are especially hard to secure, as the market rate is higher than faculty salaries.

Microfilm The university has four microfilm projectors, each in a tiny darkroom. There is also a considerable library of film. The service is politely welcomed, but is used only to a limited extent. The complaints were the usual comments as to poor focus with the edges not in focus with the center of the page, eye strain, inconvenience, and the difficulty of finding the right articles or references on hand. There are no stencils with which to copy articles.

Evaluation The University is to be commended on having maintained its academic integrity and relative freedom from political control. It apparently receives identical treatment from the Ministry of Education with other national institutions, but the higher costs of Kunming are a serious handicap. It is widely reported that the Ministry does not view the freedom of expression at Lien Ta with favor. I found free criticism of party and government policies, and a virile determination to maintain academic freedom.

Cressey Memo on Southwest University 3 Feb. 10, 1944

Despite this commendable spirit, the equipment is so poor, the student standards so low, and the preoccupation with other income producing jobs so considerable that genuine education is seriously impaired. This deterioration of education is general throughout the country. It goes down into the middle schools where college preparation is much lower than before the war. Nowhere in this or other college programs is the student held to internationally acceptable standadrds of scholarship. It is difficult to evaluate a bachelors degree, for it is deficient in quality as well as quantity. It is sometimes suggested that the present degree is worth but 60 percent of its pre war value, and at some of the weaker universities the value is much less.

This bears upon the acceptance of Chinese students by American universities. Graduates of Chinese war time colleges should certainly re-do their Senior year and possibly Junior as well, before entering upon professional study.

The unsatisfactory state of Chinese education has serious implications for the reconstruction period just ahead.

Memorandum from George B. Cressey
Cultural Relations Program, Chungking

February 10, 1944

SUBJECT National Yunnan University

ABSTRACT This is a former provincial university in Kunming

SOURCE OF DATA The University was visited twice in January 1944

SUGGESTED DISTRIBUTION Embassy, FE, RC, American accrediting institutions

MEMORANDUM

Yunnan University was started twenty years ago, and became a national university in 1938. Because of French influence in the province, the president and several of the faculty have been educated in Paris. The president is a mathematician, Dr. Ci-lan Hsieng.

There are five colleges: Arts including Political Science, Science, Engineering, Agriculture, and Medicine. The student body numbers 800, of whom 200 are women. Three-fifths of the students are from Yunnan. Standards are lower than in the National Associated Southwest University. Faculty at the latter institution commented that Yunnan University could not hold good teachers, even at comparable salaries, since its student body was inferior.

The University occupies several large and pretentious buildings on a scenic location within the city of Kunming. Financial difficulties have resulted in considerable disrepair. The campus has been twice bombed.

A visit to the four or five rooms of the Biology Department revealed 100 microscopes, nearly new and of German make, but otherwise the equipment was very poor. The rooms weredirty and untidy.

At the outlying village of Chengkung, the university has the Yunnan Station of Sociological Research, under Dr. H. D. Fein now in America, and Dr. Francis L. K. Hsu. Good research work appears to be in progress.

Yunnan University is increasing the quality of its work, and competent observers place it in the "B" class of schools.

云南大学备忘录（1944）

Memorandum from George B. Cressey
Cultural Relations Program, Chungking

May 24, 1944

SUBJECT National Wuhan University

ABSTRACT Wuhan University moved from Wuchang to Kiating in western Szechwan in 1937 with most of its library, equipment, and faculty. It maintains good morale and is one of the best schools in the country.

SOURCE OF DATA The writer spent parts of four days in Kiating in May 1944, and had numerous opportunities for faculty conferences. One general lecture was given before the student body.

SUGGESTED DISTRIBUTION Embassy, FE, SEA, American accrediting organizations.

MEMORANDUM

Wuhan University was founded in Wuchang, opposite Hankow, in 1928, but grew out of an earlier Higher Normal School. With the approach of the present war to central China, Kiating was selected after an inspection of numerous cities. It is a small but important town in western Szechwan, on a tributary of the Yangtze, with a scenic site. The availability of space in temples and Canadian Mission property was a deciding factor. The physical facilities are above the average for refugee institutions.

National Wuhan University includes Colleges of Arts, Law, Science, and Engineering. It is housed on three campuses, within fifteen minutes walk of each other. The headquarters are in a spacious Confucian temple, with an overflow in a nearby Taoist temple. Here are the Colleges of Arts and Law, with the library. Only a limited amount of remodeling and new construction has been necessary. The library numbers some 100,000 books, of which 40,000 are in English. This is one of the best libraries in Free China.

The College of Engineering is on the property of a former Canadian Middle School, with one new two story building added. Science occupies another group of buildings, largely newly built. The apparatus for Science and Engineering is exceptionally complete, so that instruction proceeds without undue difficultues for war-time China. Chemical reagents and other irreplacables are short, but still permit usual student experiments for groups of two or three working together. On each campus there are numerous temporary buildings, but they are somewhat more substantial than at most universities. It is clear that there has been competent administration and foresight.

The College of Engineering includes Departments of Civil, Electrical and Mechanical Engineering, and also Mining and Metalurgy. There is a good machine shop and foundry, which is now doing commercial work for the nearby salt fields. Castings can be made up to 3/4 ton. In the College of Science there are Departments of Chemistry, Physics, Biology and Mathematics.

国立武汉大学备忘录（1944）

Cressey Memo on Wuhan University   2   May 24, 1944

Wuhan University is reported to be free from political problems, both externally with regard to Chungking and internally as well. The spirit of the students and faculty appears to be good, and creative work is still in progress. Inflation is a serious problem, as everywhere, but not quite so acute as at some schools. This should not be interpreted as meaning that outside aid isnot needed, on the contraty for this is an institution worth preserving. Most teachers have outside income producing jobs, in some cases to a total of four. This obviously reduces the attention to teaching. The high rank of the institution is said to be related to the careful selection of the faculty when the school was first opened., and the maintanance of high standards since that time.

The faculty numbers 160, of whom 60 per cent were with the university in Wuchang. There are also 100 on the staff.

The students are reasonably well dressed and not seriously undernourished. Their academic ability and and general competence is reported locally to exceed that ofthe students in the Chengtu Christian universities. The total registration is about 1,600, of whom 200 are in Arts, 500 in Law, less than 100 in Science, and 800 in Engineering. There are also some 50 students in the Research Department which is the equivalent of a Graduate School. Only one-fourth of the students are from "down river". Nine per cent are girls.

Wuhan has the largest printing shop of any university visited, with 7 pressesand 40 workers. There is even a type foundary. The press is printing text books for local use only, so that the text problem is less serious than elsewhere.

The President is H. K. Wang, whose health is not too good, and the Dean and active administrative official is Chu Kwang-tsien

Wihan University is generally conceded among Chinese educators to rank within the best four universities. This visit substantiated that opinion. The extent to which standards have deteriorated due to the war is difficult to measure, probably less than elsewhere but nevertheless considerable. It was strongly contended that the work in Mathematics and a few other departments was fully up to world academic specifications.

Memorandum from George B. Cressey
Cultural Relations Program, Chungking

May 24, 1944

SUBJECT <u>National Szechwan University</u>

ABSTRACT Szechwan University is a large institution of moderate standing in the outskirts of Chengtu.

SOURCE OF DATA The University was visited on April 2[illegible], with an opportunity for meeting some of the faculty at tea, and a lecture to the student body.

SUGGESTED DISTRIBUTION Embassy, FE, SEA, American educational organizations

Memorandum

National Szechwan University has a large but somewhat barren campus along the river a few miles south of Chengtu. There are four large buildings in Chinese style, but they are poorly kept. The campus lacks trees and landscaping. The buildings were built in 1936.

The University returned to this campus last year after three years of refugeeing at Omei Hsien., a few miles to the west.

There are Colleges of Law, Agriculture, Education, Arts, and Science, listed in the order of their enrollment. The total registration is 3000, of whom 1300 are in a Freshman College. One tenth are girls. The teaching staff numbers ~~25~~ 250, of whom 100 are of professorial rank. Some 95% of the latter have studied abroad.

The library contains 100,000 volumes, including 20,000 in foreign languages which are said to be well selected. Some of these are inherited from earlier institutions out of which Szechwan University developed.

National Szechwan University appears to occupy a secondary position among Chengtu universities somewhat comparable to that of Yunnan University in Kunming and Chungking University at Shapingpa. Superior students prefer to enter elsewhere.

The president is Huang Chi-lu (not met), and the Dean is Mr. Yuan. A Miss Marion E. Cleveland serves as English Secretary to the President.

国立四川大学备忘录（1944）

Memorandum from George B. Cressey
Cultural Relations Program, Chungking

May 24, 1944

SUBJECT Chengtu Christian Universities

ABSTRACT Five American supported universities share the campus of West China Union University, namely Nanking, Lingnan, Ginling and Cheloo. There is close cooperation but no federation. The excellent campus, academic facilities, large foreign faculty, and intelligent student body make this one of the outstanding educational centers of Free China. Education continues here more normally than elsewhere.

SOURCE OF DATA The writer spent ten days on the campus, from April 18 through 28, with many opportunities for conference. I met each of the five presidents separately and also together, talked with many members of the faculty, and gave numerous lectures before the students.

SUGGESTED DISTRIBUTION Embassy, FE, SEA, Associated Boards for Christian Colleges in China, Foundations and other interested agencies.

MEMORANDUM

The Campus West China Union University occupies a very attractive and spacious site just outside Chengtu. It is known in Chinese as Hua Hsi Ta Hsueh. Most of the support comes from United States sources, but Canadian influence is strong and there are also Britishers. In addition to the university plant there is a large hospital, a middle school, and a Canadian School for foreign children.

The academic rating of the five universities and their place among other Chinese schools is approximately as follows: University of Nanking, Class A, Yenching University, Class B, West China Union University and Ginling College, Class C, and Cheloo University (Shantung Christian College) in a lower category.

The combined foreign community numbers some 75, which represents a considerable decline from a few years ago. Dozens of the Chinese faculty are western returned students. I found many of these people, both Chinese and foreign, to be very keen, and I had numerous penetrating discussions. At the same time it must be added that some of the foreign faculty are of mediocre academic ability and personality.

At the moment, this campus represents the major agency in China for international cultural good will. It deserves a larger measure of official and private support from the United States.

中国主要教会大学备忘录（1944）

-2-

The campus is well laid out with foresight and imagination. There are a dozen large two and three story buildings in Chinese architecture, plus many smaller structures. Well kept lawns, many trees, and proper maintainance give the campus an air of academic maturity lacking in any other university in Free China. The West China physical plant stands next to Yenching and Lingnan as the third best plant among the Christian schools.

The students are exceptionally well dressed, many of the men in western style. They obviously come from wealthy and official families. Dozens of bicycles give a distinctive air. The financial level does not imply equally high scholastic abilities, but it is nevertheless clear that these students are a superior group. It is also worthy of note that wealthy families have chosen to send their children to Christian universities. As will be indicated later, there are differences from one college to another.

One may walk across the campus and from the visible scene it would not be apparent that there was a war or inflation. This is only a superficial impression, for the consequences of each are real.

The enrollment and staff are as follows, for the Fall Semester 1943.

Institution	Students	Faculty and Staff full time	part time
West China Union	1150 (1/3 girls)	302	34
Nanking (incl. College of Science at Chungking)	1100 (50 girls)	249	21
Cheloo	460 (1/3 girls)	70	6
Yenching	380 (1/3 girls)	86	17
Ginling	280 (all girls)	68	11
	3370 (700 girls)	777	

The five Christian universities maintain their separate existence, but share the same campus and facilities. The Presidents meet weekly for conference. Since the original facilities were inadequate, a new and excellent Chemistry building has been added by some of the "down river" schools, and Lingnan has constructed a large wing of the hospital plant for science classes. Nanking and Cheloo have built numerous smaller buildings, all of which will revert to West China after the war.

A larger measure of cooperation would bring large financial savings, and probably higher standards, by eliminating duplicate courses and one third of the existing staff. Administrative overhead is now high, and might thereby be reduced. The normal teaching load has been but nine hours, but was raised last fall to 10 and 12.

-3-

Library facilities include West China's collection of 120,000 Chinese and 80,000 foreign volumes, Nanking's 37,425 books and 26,066 periodicals, plus a few tens of thousands of Ginling books. Cheloo and Yenching were unable to bring their libraries. This is by far the best library anywhere in Free China, and it is very well housed.

West China has an outstanding museum, with 26,000 objects, under the competent direction of Harvard trained Wu Teh-chun and a staff of four others. There are large halls for pottery and for Tibetan materials, plus numerous alcoves for bronzes, sculpture, and tribes peoples. The museum was founded in 1922 and would be a credit in any country.

Any description of the university must include reference to the West China Border Research Society, a separate organization with an international reputation. They have published a journal for many years.

An Institute of Comparative Cultures has just been organized under the leadership of Professor William Fenn, Professor Cheng Teh-kun, and Dr. E.H. Cressy of Chungking. This promises to be a project which will contribute to better understanding between the United States and Asia, and will probably justify official American support. For the present it is proposed to organize a group of courses and integration seminar, sponsor lectures, and exchange professors and students. Later it is hoped to publish, e.g. a popular history of Chinese literature in English, a good history of the United States in Chinese, etc. An outstanding American visiting professor of mature ability in the field of the humanities would be much welcomed.

University of Nanking The University of Nanking was founded fifty years ago and has had a fruitful record of Chinese-American cooperation. The work in agriculture and forestry has been especially notable. The enrollment in 1936 was 900, the largest of the Christian schools. Nanking has been the most Chinese in its administration, and relations are friendly. In contrast to the strong pre-war foreign staff, including numerous visiting professors from Cornell, there is now but one full time teacher. The Chinese administration desires more foreign teachers, and feel sufficiently secure in their position so that they do not fear foreign domination.

The College of Agriculture, which includes forestry and agricultural economics, is the best unit. The College of Science is partly on the Chiu Ching campus in Chungking. In order to provide a war-time income it is partly in business with more attention toward the engineering side than to pure science. Its work in visual education through moving pictures, in Chengtu, is outstanding. The College of Arts is at low ebb. English is its major contribution, along with History, Political Science, and Sociology. Unfortunately half of the students are in Economics,

-4-

which turns out bank clerks. The Chengtu colleges unite in English but operate four departments of Economics, each the largest in its university.

Despite lowered standards, Nanking is the strongest university on the campus, and in the same top class with Amoy, Wuhan and Lienta.

The problems of a refugee institution are illustrated in the dormitories. Whereas West China students are placed four to a room in good buildings, Nanking students are crowded eight to a room in temporary buildings.

The president is Dr. Y.G. Chen, who will go to the United States this summer as the guest of the Departmentof State.

Yenching University When Yenching was on its campus outside Peiping, it was the leading foreign supported school in China. After Pearl Harbor it was obliged to suspend operations, and 42 foreigners were interned. The University reopened in Chengtu two years ago, with no equipment and only a few of its original staff or students.

Yenching is torn between the desire to restore its former prestige and superiority complex, and the realities of insufficient funds, the lack of an able faculty, and the absence of equipment. Since it was the last to arrive in Chengtu it has had to fit into whatever space was available. Most of the work is inside the city, a considerable distance from the other institutions, on the campus of a former Methodist Girls Middle School and an adjoining Confucian temple. The College of Science has a new building on the West China campus where Lingnan has built a large addition to the hospital of which it will have the use during the war. Chemistry courses are given in the West China Chemistry building, and English instruction is also given jointly.

The faculty includes 35 who have come from Peiping, and several strong newcomers are being added. A total of 350 students have migrated, but many of these have now graduated or joined the Interpretors School.

Yenching continues its colleges of Arts, Public Affairs, and Science, each with the required minimum of three departments. There is an urgent need for foreign teachers.

The acting President is Y.P. Mei.

West China Union University West China is in the midst of growing pains. Although the campus was laid out for a large institution, the pre-war enrollment was but 300. This has now grown to 1150. Since there were no important universities nearby, there was little academic competition and standards were quite low. Many of the foreign faculty seem to have been of inadequate ability in academic fields. The arrival of the "down river" refugee universities has brought many changes. The increase in enrollment is partly from a competitive desire to be as large as the others. Academic standards have been materially raised, while at the same time the guest schools have had to lower theirs. Several good Chinese teachers have been added.

Post war conditions will require the addition of new blood not brought up in the West China tradition. There are no prospects that West China will become a Class A school for some years. Before the war the institution was dominated by westerners with more foreign control than in most such institutions. Few Chinese leaders were developed, and there was considerable restlessness. This condition has been completely changed, and Westerners now have even less than their proper voice.

There are three colleges, Art has been the weakest in the past but is now expanding. Science is strong in Chemistry and Pharmacy. Medicine and Dentistry are exceptionally good for their position in interior China; Canadian interests dominate.

Since West China has its roots in Chengtu, its faculty has the advantage in the matter of outside income producing jobs, and in the assignment to campus residences.

The president is Lincoln Tsang.

<u>Ginling College</u> Ginling includes a College of Arts and a College of Science. Since it does not meet the Ministry requirement of three colleges, it is not listed as a University. It occupies the buildings of the former Canadian School for western children.

The academic standards at Nanking were good, since the entering students came from superior girls middle schools with strong foreign staffs. Since such Freshmen are no longer available, Ginling standards are now somewhat lower. In fact it is universally true in war time China that the deterioration of middle school work has pulled down university possibilities.

Ginling prides itself on personal contacts, made possible by the large staff of 68 teachers and assistants for 280 students. This has conspicuous advantages, but the sentimental interest is reported to make the school unwilling to flunk students or postpone graduation.

The available equipment of Ginling College is very limited, but to preserve its self respect it continues to offer courses already available elsewhere on the campus irrespective of the ability of its own staff to give the work. Instruction in music is especially good.

The president is Dr. Wu Yi-fan, one of the most able women in China.

-6-

Cheloo University This school was once known as Shantung Christian College, and before the war was located outside Tsinan. Early in the war, the then president, Mr. Liu, came to Chengtu in order to open a refugee institution. The foreign faculty, however, felt that there was no danger in Shantung and decided to keep the school open there. This provided misunderstandings which are suggestive of long standing problems within the faculty and administration.

Cheloo University in Chengtu has only a minimum of equipment, and must thus lean heavily on West China. There are numerous internal political problems, and the institution has had some 15 presidents and acting presidents in 20 years. The College of Medicine includes some good men, otherwise the faculty is weak.

The acting President is Edgar Tang.

Memorandum from George B. Cressey
Cultural Relations Program, Chungking

June 1, 1944

SUBJECT Sun Yat-sen University

ABSTRACT Sun Yat-sen University is one of the largest schools in Free China, but its standards are low. Its various colleges are in and near Pingshih in northern Kwangtung.

SOURCE OF DATA The writer visited the university from March 1 to 4, 1944

SUGGESTED DISTRIBUTION Embassy, FE, SEA, Associated Boards, etc.

Memorandum

Sun Yat-sen University is often known as Chung Shan Ta Hsueh. It formerly had a large and well equipped campus near Canton, but standards have greatly deteriorated.

There were the following colleges and students in the fall of 1943.

College of Science, at Pingshih		348	students
College of Science, at Pingshih		217	students
College of Engineering, 2 km. from Pingshih		884	"
College of Law, 2 km. from Pingshih		831	"
College of Agriculture, 20 km. distant, in southern Hunan		404	"
College of Medicine, at Lochang, Kwangtung		284	"
College of Education, 10 km. south		556	"
Graduate School, at Pingshih		20	"
			3544 students
Sub Freshmen	about	300	"
Middle School	about	300	"

The University moved to Kunming in 1938, and to Pingshih in 1939. Very little of the original equipment was saved, but there are 400 cases of books and apparatus in Kunming which cannot be transported. The present facilities are seriously inadequate.

Standards are admittedly low. The faculty do not meet classes regularly, nor do students attend. Examinations are perfunctory or omitted. Degrees are almost automatic. Entrance examinations are taken by between 8,000 and 15,000, reports vary, of whom 800 are accepted. The latter figure is controlled by dormitory accommodations, which are exceedingly poor and without supervision. The tuition is free, as at all government schools, and there is a large contribution toward board, especially with engineering students. There is no athletic field and not one piano. The Student Christian Center, under the Y.M.C.A. is meeting a major need here as elsewhere, notably with National Central and Kwangsi University.

中山大学备忘录（1944）

Cressey Memo on Sun Yat-sen University 2 June 1, 1944

The faculty now numbers 350, relatively few of whom speak English or appear to have studied abroad. Before the war the University had several German visiting professors. Prior to the removal from Canton in 1938, the faculty numbered 220, of whom 65 per cent moved to Kunming. Due to resignations and increases in the total number, but 140 of the original teaching body remain. Many of the faculty have one or more outside jobs, and are doing a very poor job of teaching.

Sun Yat-sen University is noted for serious political troubles, both internal and external. Deans and even presidents secure their posts by organizing student factions and cliques. Student troubles frequently arise prior to the examinations, while the faculty present difficulties before the signing of the annual contracts. Considerable pressure is brought on the university to accept sub-standard students, and pass them.

The university is generally regarded by competent critics in this part of China as one of the poorest of the major schools, yet its budget is the third or fourth largest among the National Universities.

There have been three presidents in four years. The current head is Pres. Chin Chen-ching, trained in Japan. The university dean is Teng Chi-yi.

Memorandum from George B. Cressey
Cultural Relations Program, Chungking

June 1, 1944

SUBJECT (Fukien Christian University

ABSTRACT The university has a refugee campus at Shaowu, to which most of the original equipment has been transferred. The spirit is excellent and the academic work quite good.

SOURCE OF DATA The writer spent March 28 to April 1 in Shaowu

DISTRIBUTION Embassy, FE, SEA, Associated Boards, etc.

Memorandum

Fukien Christian University, known in Chinese as Hsi Ho Ta Hsueh, is probably the only refugee institution which still has access to its original campus and equipment. The original plant, in Foochow, has been unmolested and it is still possible to bring up supplies and books. Shaowu is a small town in northwestern Fukien, with water and road connections with Foochow, but very much isolated from the rest of China. This is the most inaccessible university visited by the writer, 11 trucks and busses away from the railroad at Kukong, and "20 beds" distant from Chungking. Despite the isolation, the contact with the relatively modernized city of Foochow provides certain supplies not so readily available in the interior.

Fukien Christian University is a joint project of the Methodist, Congregational, and American Reformed churches in America, with some cooperation from the China Inland Mission. There are ten foreigners on the staff, who contribute materially to the standards and spirit. The significance of foreign personnel is strikingly obvious in war time Chinese Universities. Too many returned students tend to go down hill intellectually without this stimulus.

The school moved to Shaowu because of the availability of mission middle school and hospital property. These are at opposite ends of the town, some fifteen minutes walk apart. The College of Science is in the hospital and adjoining residences, while the Colleges of Arts and Agriculture are housed in the middle school and associated residence property plus a few new buildings. The physical facilities are quite adequate, and the equipment likewise. The library has 90,000 volumes here, plus an additional 40,000 in Foochow.

The faculty numbers 63, all of them full time. Two thirds are returned students. In the spring semester of 1944 there were 474 students, of whom 89 were women. Sixty per cent come from Fukien

The College of Agriculture includes departments of agronomy, horticulture, economics, rural education, and industrial arts. The students number 212. Active research work is under way with several experimental farms, and an intelligent program. Among other things, the university has developed two new varieties of rice, with 25 and 40 per cent increased yields.

福建协和大学备忘录（1944）

Cressey Memo on Fukien Christian University 2 June 1, 1944

The College of Arts, with 131 students, includes departments of Chinese Language and Literature, History, Foreign Languages (English and German, once Japanese and French), and Education which will end in two years due to the Ministry of Education rulings about Education in private universities, but which is in effect being transferred to Agriculture under the heading of Rural Education.

The College of Science offers work in Chemistry, Biology, and Physics. Chemical reagents are short, but still permit two students to work together on the same experiment. There are 140 students. Biology has 50 microscopes, and a very large herbrarium and bird collection.

The President is Lin Chin-jun, the Dean of Science is Wang Tiao-hsin also head of Chemistry, the Dean of Agriculture is Edwin Chen, head of Economics. These two departments, together with Western Languages, are the leading fields.

Student spirit appears to be excellent, with the best singing and patriotic exercises of any university visited.

Textbooks are available on a rental basis for almost all classes, and the University has its own printing shop. Freshmen must usually share one testbook for two students if majors in the department, and with three if non majors. Advanced courses have one text for each student. This is in great contrast to many schools where there are no texts or even mimeographed outlines for most courses.

Memorandum from George B. Cressey
Cultural Relations Program, Chungking

June 1, 1944

SUBJECT Soochow University

ABSTRACT Soochow has just moved to a temporary campus in Northern Kwangtung, adjoining that of Lingnan University. The equipment is exceedingly inadequate.

SOURCE OF INFORMATION The writer visited the campus on February 29, 1944

SUGGESTED DISTRIBUTION Embassy, FE, SEA/Associated Boards, etc.

Memorandum

Soochow University had a maximum pre-war enrollment of 1300, placing it next to Yenching among Christian universities. During the early part of the war it operated in Shanghai, then moved to Shaowu and to Sin jen miao in northern Kwangtung, near Kukong. The College of Law operates in Chungking, in association with the College of Commerce of the University of Shanghai.

The present campus of Soochow includes half a dozen temporary one story buildings on an open hillside. The site was selected since it is fifteen minutes walk from Lingnan University. Almost no teaching equipment is available, nor does Lingnan have any surplus to offer. There are two microscopes and a few chemicals, glassware is on order. There is no library.

The enrollment is 120, including 30 to 40 women. All of them are Freshmen and Sophomores, and only a handful are old Soochow students. Of the 1800 applicants last fall, but 70 were admitted and but 7 met the pre war standards. The College of Law has an additional 180 students.

The faculty of 18 compares favorably with Lingnan, especially in Science. Most of them are returned students, and new to Soochow so that there is no academic coherence. Five are from Great Britain, four from the United States, and one each from Germany, Japan and France.

Standards are said to be relatively good, but in the almost complete absence of facilities, the academic offerings are far below standard. The only two classes which make any pretext of having textbooks are English and Chinese.

It is still possible for student records to be mailed out from the office in Shanghai.

The acting president is T. L. Shen

东吴大学备忘录（1944）

Memorandum from George B. Cressey
Cultural Relations Program, Chungking

June 1, 1944

SUBJECT <u>Lingnan University</u>

ABSTRACT Lingnan has a temporary campus in northern Kwangtung, with limited equipment but with good students and fine spirit.

SOURCE OF INFORMATION The writer visited the campus Feb. 28-30, 1944

SUGGESTED DISTRIBUTION Embassy, FE, SEA, Associated Boards, etc.

Memorandum

Lingnan University, once known as Canton Christian College, was one of the best American founded institutions prior to the war, with excellent facilities and a scholarly faculty. When the war reached Canton they moved to Hongkong, and from there to the tiny hamlet of Sin jen miao, a few hours by rail north of Kukong, Kwangtung in May1942. Most of the equipment was left in Hongkong, but it is still possible to bring out material through the Japanese lines; four such cases have just arrived.

The university has half a dozen temporary buildings of fairly substantial construction, but most of the work is in bamboo mat sheds. The campus is in the midst of a grove of large trees, and the physical plant makes a good impression. The working equipment is far below standard. The library has a set of the Encyclopedia Britannica, but the few other books are gifts or loans from alumni and missionary friends.

The enrollment is 510, of whom 43 are women. The College of Medicine is at Kukong, and the College of Agriculture is at Pingshih. The College of Aarts and Science, and the College of Engineering are at Sin jen miao. At the last entrance examinations there were 2500 applicants, of whom 154 were accepted. Lingnan students appear unusually bright, and were very responsibe to the writers lectures. Most of them are from Hongkong and Canton, foreign style dress is prevalent among the men. Their economic level is distinctly above that of the surrounding universities.

The faculty numbers 50, of whom 10 are full professors. The president is Y. L. Lee

Canton Union Theological College, with 30 students, is nearby and cooperates. It is under Mr. J. S. Kunkle.

岭南大学备忘录（1944）

Memorandum from George B. Cressey
Cultural Relations Program, Chungking

June 1, 1944

SUBJECT Amoy University

ABSTRACT Amoy University is temporarily located at Changting, Fukien, with unusually good temporary facilities and superior equipment and faculty. It is one of the best schools in Free China.

SOURCE OF DATA March 12 - 15, 1944 were spent at the University

SUGGESTED DISTRIBUTION Embassy, FE, SEA, Associated Boards, etc.

Memorandum

Amoy University is one of the four best institutions in Free China. It is known in Chinese as Sha Men Ta Hsueh. It has good traditions, excellent library and equipment, a strong faculty and good students, able leadership, and a fine spirit. The buildings are semi-permanent and quite adequate, a few have been lost by bombing. The dormitories are among the best in China, with no more than four to a room. The laboratories are surprisingly well equipped, active and orderly. Engineering has good shops. Biology is the best supplied department, but has the fewest students.

The university was founded by a wealthy Amoy citizen who gave some four million dollars for the university and middle school, a separate institution. There was no endowment within China but income was derived from rubber planations and other enterprises in Malaya. When this source of support was cut off, the university was obliged to become a National University in order to continue. The considerable increase in the number of National Universities during the war is probably due to situations such as this rather than an active campaign on the part of the Ministry of Education to absorb private schools.

Amoy moved to Changting, in interior southwestern Fukien, in December 1937; and has most of its original equipment. Chemicals were adequate for laboratory work for six years, but are now becoming short. Hence General Chemistry is limited to departmental majors, thus excluding engineering students. The library has 150,000 volumes, otherwise stated to be 90,000 actually in Changting, and is interestingly housed in an old temple. The university loans texts for all freshmen courses, and is preparing to print Sophomore texts. For advanced courses, the library has ten to fifteen copies on reserve.

There are four colleges and thirteen departments. The College of Arts, with 50 students, has departments of Chinese Literature, History, and Education. The College of Science and Engineering, 400 students, has departments of Physics-Mathematics, Chemistry, Biology, Civil Engineering, Mechanical-Elictrical Engineering, and will add Aeronautical Engineering next fall. In the College of Law there are 200 students in the departments of Law, Political Science, and Economics. The College of Commerce, enrolling 150 students, offers Banking and Accounting. The total registration

厦门大学备忘录（1944）

[redacted]ssey Memo on Amoy University 2 June 1,

in 1944 is 860, of whom 76 are women. Considerable pressure is brought on the university to accept more students, but the emphasis is on small numbers and quality. Mechanical and Electrical Engineering is the most popular department, following by Economics which is often first elsehwere. The s tudents are 50 per cent from Fukien, 15 per cent from Kiangsi which is nearby, and 25 per cent from Chekiang and Kiangsu combined.

The faculty includes 50 "recognized" professors, e.g. certified by the Ministry of Education, and the entire staff numbers 200. Three volumes of faculty research were published by the university in 1943, one in English, all printed locally.

Inflation is very serious here as elsewhere. Rice which cost $8 is now $2400. an increase of 300 times. When the university arrived in Changting, the local shopkeepers were amazed at the prosperity of the teachers and said "These people must be getting $30 a month, they live so well," whereas the usual salary was actually about $240. Today it is recognized that the teachers are one of the poorest groups in town. Whereas the President's pre-war salary would equal all of the coolie pay roll, the salary and rice allowances of the latter now equal 20 to 30 times the salary of the president.

The president is Dr. A. Pen-tung Sah, who has been invited to come to the United States by the Division of Science Education and Art of the Department of State. The dean is Hsieh Yu-ming.

Memorandum from George B. Cressey
Cultural Relations Program, Chungking

June 7, 1944

SUBJECT List of Chinese Institutions of Higher Education

ABSTRACT China has 141 institutions of higher education, as follows:

National Universities	23)	each university must consist
Private Universities	18)	of three or more colleges
National Colleges	18	
Provincial Colleges	13	
Private Colleges	20	
National Technical Schools	16	
Provincial Technical Schools	19	
Private Technical Schools	14	
Total	141	

SOURCE OF DATA Supplied by Mr. Wu Chun-sheng, Director of Higher Education of the Ministry of Education, June 6, 1944

SUGGESTED DISTRIBUTION Embassy, FE, SEA, Associated Boards, Foundations, etc.

Memorandum

A List of Institutions of Higher Education

(1944)

National Universities

Names	Location	Enrolment	Expenditures
National Central University	Shapingpa, Chungking	3,740	$ 12,556,259
National South West Associated University	Kunming	2,381	11,638,699
National North Western University	Chengku, Shensi	1,180	2,979,123
National Sun Yat-sen University	Pingshek, Kwangtung	3,573	9,988,123
National Chiao-tung University	Chungking	909	5,205,747
National Tung-chi University	Nanchi, Szechuan	1,122	4,073,720
National Chinan University	Kien-yang, Fukien	1,006	2,506,410
National Wuhan University	Loshan, Szechwan	1,549	5,538,257
National Chekiang University	Tsun-yi, Kweichow	1,685	7,224,925
National Szechwan University	Chengtu, Szechwan	2,305	6,556,405

中国大专院校概况（1944）

-2-

Name	Location	Enrolment	Expenditures
National Northeastern University	Santai, Szechwan	764	$ 2,330,228
National Hunan University	Shengki, Hunan	1,262	3,672,598
National Amoy University	Changting, Fukien	358	2,896,204
National Yunnan University	Kunming, Yunnan	684	6,097,734
National Chung-Cheng University	Tai Ho, Kiangsi	1,366	3,575,932
National Kwangsi University	Kweilin, Kwangsi	1,822	5,320,726
National Futan University	Peipei, Szechwan	1,732	3,792,000
National Honan University	Sunghsien, Honan	1,040	2,620,000
National Kweichow University	Kweiyang, Kweichow	683	4,256,654
National Chungking University	Shapingpa, Chung-kking	1,244	4,020,000
National Shansi University	I-Chwan, Shensi	223	1,600,000
National Ying Shih University	Chingning, Chekiang	597	3,053,711
National Chiao-tung University, Kweichow Branch	Pingyueh, Kweichow	794	2,301,560

Private Universities

Name	Location	Enrolment	Expenditures
University of Nanking	Chengtu, Szechwan	1,016	
Tatung University	Shanghai	1,330	
Kuo-Min University of Kwangtung	Kaiping, Kwangtung	1,423	
University of Shanghai	Shanghai	863	
Kwang-Hua University	Chengtu, Szechwan	1,255	
Great China University	Kweiyang, Kweichow	740	
Yenching University	Chengtu, Szechwan	386	
Foo Jen (Catholic University) University	Peiping	2,109	
Soochow University	Ku-Kiang, Kwangtunf	132	
Chung Hwa University of Wu-Chang	Chungking	549	

-3-

Name	Location	Enrolment	Expenditures
Lingnan University	Ku-Kiang, Kwangtung	576	
Franco-China University	Kunming	352	
Fukien Union University	Shaowu, Fukien	474	
Cheeloo University	Chengtu, Szechwan	464	
University of Canton	Kukiang, Kwangtung	1,095	
Cheng-Tan (Aurora) University	Shanghai	537	
West China Union University	Chengtu, Szechwan	1,080	
Central China University	Tali, Yunnan	150	

National Independent Colleges

Name	Location	Enrolment	Expenditures
National College of Commerce	Chien Chen, Hunan	542	$ 889,514
National Medical College of Shanghai	Koloshan, Chungking	269	1,564,218
National Chung-Cheng College of Medicine	Yü ngsien, Kiangsi	242	1,278,614
National Medical College of Kweiyang	Kweiyang, Kweichow	167	1,382,433
National Medical College of Kiangsu	Peipei, Szechwan	217	1,496,180
National North Western College of Medicine	Nancheng, Shensi	266	1,351,842
National Hsiang Yan College of Medicine	Kweiyang, Kweichow	206	1,429,571
National Teacher's College	Anhua, Hunnan	716	2,809,031
National North Western Teacher's College	Lanchow, Kansu	845	3,463,915
National North Western College of Engineering	Chengku, Shensi	1,058	3,321,127
National North Western College of Agriculture	Wukung, Shensi	579	2,829,641
National Teacher's College of Women	Pesha, Kiangtsing, Szechwan	556	2,019,314
National College of Social Education	Peishan, Szechwan	538	1,671,200

-4-

Name	Location	Enrolment	Expenditures
National Teacher's College of Kweiyang	Kweiyang, Kweichow	268	$ 1,651,620
National Teacher's College of Kweilin	Kweilin, Kwangsi	380	1,638,772
National Teacher's College of Hupeh	Enshih, Hupeh	316	1,284,774
National College of Kansu	Lanchow	235	918,116
National Peiyang College of Engineering	Taihsun, Chekiang	198	

Provincial Independent Colleges

Name	Location	Enrolment	Expenditures
Provincial College of Sinkiang	Tihua, Sinkiang	45	
Provincial Hsiang-Ching College of Commerce	Kukiang, Kwangtung	415	
Provincial College of Kwangtung	Kukiang, Kwangtung	402	
Provincial College of Education of Szechwan	Chungking	241	
Provincial College of Medicine of Fukien	Shasien, Fukien	260	
Provincial College of Medicine of Kwangsi	Kweilin, Kwangsi	161	
Provincial College of Agriculture of Fukien	Yung-an, Fukien	208	
Provincial College of Agriculture of Hupeh	Enshih, Hupeh	211	
Provincial College of Kiangsu	Shan Yuan, Fukien	266	
Provincial College of Anhwei	Li-Hwang, Anhwei	548	
Provincial Frontier College of Shangtung, Kiangsu, Anhwei, Honan	Linchuan, Anhwei	150	
Provincial Medical College of Hupeh	Enshih, Hupeh		
Provincial Women's College of Sinkiang	Ti-hua, Sinkiang		

-5-

Private Independent Colleges

Name	Location	Enrolment	Expenditures
Peiping Union Medical College (School of Nursing)	Chengtu, Szechwan		
Shanghai College of Law and Political Science	Tunki, Anhwei	224	
Nantung College	Yung Chia, Chekiang	480	
Chung-Kuo College	Peiping	1,410	
Shanghai College of Law	Shiu-lin, Anhwei	320	
Chaoyang College	Pahsien, Szechwan	698	
Ginling College	Chengtu, Szechwan	280	
Fukien College	Min-Ching, Fukien	196	
Chen-Ming College of Arts	Shanghai	133	
Min-Kuo College of Peiping	Ninhsiang, Hunan	312	
Hwa-Nan College	Nanping, Fukien	113	
Tientsin College of Commerce and Engineering	Tientsin	377	
Women's Medical College of Shanghai	Shanghai	33	
Tung-Teh College of Medicine	Shanghai	478	
Tung-Nan College of Medicine	Shanghai	270	
Kwang-Hwa College of Medicine	Macao	558	
Hangchow College	Sao-Wu, Kwangtung	233	
South China College	Meihsien, Kwangtung	301	
College of Rural Reconstruction of China	Pahsien, Szechwan	122	
Szechwan-Sikang College of Agriculture and Engineering	Chengtu, Szechwan	231	

National Technical Schools

Name	Location	Enrolment	Expenditures
National School of Music	Ching Mou Kuan, Chungking	145	$ 1,033,020

-6-

Name	Location	Enrolment	Expenditures
National School of Fine Arts	Shapingpa, Szechwan	229	$ 1,014,372
National Central School of Engineering	Shapingpa, Szechwan	504	718,000
National School of Pharmacy	Koloshan, Chungking	208	1,168,163
National School of Dentistry	Chengtu, Szechwan	50	460,912
National Teacher's School of Physical Exercise	Peipei, Szechwan	147	527,534
National Central School of Technology	Loshan, Szechwan	308	1,763,884
National Northwestern School of Technology	Lanchow, Kansu	298	1,962,934
National School of Technology of Sikang	Sichang, Szechwan	261	1,943,619
National School of Drama	Kiangan, Szechwan	105	910,576
National Teacher's School of Physical Education	Kiangtsing, Szechwan	104	782,000
National Frontier School	Chungking	186	
National School of Oriental Languages	Chengkung, Yunnan	121	745,520
National Fukien School of Music	Yung-An, Fukien	141	454,800
National Northwestern School of Medicine	Lanchow, Kansu	175	503,600
National School of Hydraulic Engineering	Cheng-Ping, Honan	52	602,000

Provincial Technical Schools

Name	Location	Enrolment	Expenditures
Provincial School of Medicine and Pharmacy of Chekiang	Ninhai, Chekiang	37	
Provincial School of Engineering of Kiangsi	Sautu, Liangsi	267	
Provincial School of Veterinary Science of Kiangsi	Taiho, Kiangsi	42	
Provincial School of Medicine of Kiangsi	Kanchow, Kiangsi	227	
Provincial School of Medicine of Shangtung	Wanhsien, Szechwan	126	

-7-

Name	Location	Enrolment	Expenditures
Provincial School of Medicine of Shensi	Sian, Shansi	196	
Provincial School of Seri-Culture of Kiangsu	Kiating, Szechwan	40	
Provincial Teacher's School of Fukien	Yungan, Fukien	262	
Provincial School of Agriculture of Hunan	Nanyao, Hunan	149	
Provincial School of Engineering of Hunan	Nanyao, Hunan	260	
Provincial School of Commerce of Hunan	Nanyao, Hunan	222	
Provincial School of Fine Arts of Szechwan	Chengtu, Szechwan	159	
Provincial School of Commerce of Shensi	Sian, Shansi	306	
Provincial School of Physical Education	Chengtu, Szechwan		
Provincial School of English Language of Yunnan	Kunming		
Provincial School of Agri-culture of Kiangsi	Taiho, Kiangsi		
Provincial School of En-gineering of Kwangtung			
Provincial School of Fine Arts of Kwangtung	Kukiang, Kwangtung	105	
Provincial School of Accounting of Szechwan	Chengtu, Szechwan	92	

Private Technical Schools

Name	Location	Enrolment	Expenditures
Wusih School of Chinese Classics	Kweilin, Kwangsi	277	
Wen-Hwei (Bonne) Library School	Chungking	34	
Wuchang School of Fine Arts	Kianghsing, Szechwan	129	
Far East School of Physical Education	Shanghai	68	
Shanghai School of Fine Arts	Shanghai	179	

- 8 -

Name	Location	Enrolment	Expenditures
Hsin Hwa School of Fine Arts	Shanghai	102	
Li Hsin School of Accounting	Peipei, Szechwan	301	
Soochow School of Fine Arts	Shanghai	85	
Min-Hsien School of Agriculture and Engineering	Kiangtang, Szechwan		
North Western School of Pharmacy	Sian, Shensi	70	
Shanghai English School	Shanghai	62	
West China School of Commerce and Engineering	Chungking	164	
Chiu Ching School of Cpmmerce	Chungking	158	
School of Chinese Classics	Pingshek, Kwangtung		

Memorandum from George B. Cressey
Cultural Relations Program, Chungking

May 27, 1944

SUBJECT Evaluation of Chinese Universities

ABSTRACT War time education has deteriorated by some 50 per cent. The four leading universities are National Southwestern (Lienta), Nanking, Amoy and Wuhan

SOURCE OF DATA This memorandum is based on extensive travel, personal investigation, and many conferences.

SUGGESTED DISTRIBUTION Embassy, FE, SEA, Associated Boards, otherwise

MEMORANDUM RESTRICTED

War time education in China has seriously deteriorated. At National Southwestern in Kunming I was told that up to last year the quality of the work had depreciated by 25 per cent and that this year had brought a further 15 per cent decline. At most schools the standards have been lowered even more, so that a degree from an institution such as Sun Yat-sen University which did excellent work in Canton is now nearly worthless. On the other hand some universities, noteably Wuhan and Fukien Christian University insist that their scholastic work, at least in some departments, is fully up to pre war standards. On the whole it may be correct to say that university work has depreciated by 50 per cent.

The following evaluation is based upon personal visitation, except where noted, plus repeated questioning of Chinese educators as to their own listing by rank. The order can only be subjective, and is merely relative within China.

Class A universities

1. National Southwestern Associated University, known as Lienta, Kunming. A distinguished faculty which preserves the traditions of Tsinghua, Nankai, and PeipingNational, high scholastic standards, poor equipment, declining morale due to serious inflation.

2. University of Nanking, Chengtu
Splendid campus, good student body, high standards

3. Amoy University, Changting, Fukien
excellent equipment and leadership, good spirit

4. Wuhan University, Kiating, Szechwan
excellent equipment, good faculty and students, high standards

Class B universities

5. Chekiang University, Tsunyi, Kweichow
not visited but highly regarded, frequent moves have resulted in the loss of much equipment

6. National Central University, Shapingpa near Chungking
some able faculty but serious political problems both within and without, equipment only fair, often regarded as Class A but doubtful.

中国高等院校评估排名（1944）

Cressey Memo on Evaluation of Universities 2 May 27, 1944

7. Fukien Christian University, Shaowu, Fukien
small and isolated but doing excellent work, very good spirit, complete equipment and access to original campus in Foochow

8. Yenching University, Chengtu
recently reopened but rapidly rebuilding, good traditions

Class C universities (acceptable but marginal, some others not visited might be included, e.g. Hunan and Tungchi)

9. West China Union University, Chengtu
excellent campus and facilities, standards rising

10. Lingnan University, Sinjenmiao near Kukong, Kwangtung
very limited equipment but good students and spirit

11. Chungking University, Shapingpa near Chungking

12. Yunnan University, Kunming

13. Ginling College, Chengtu
some advantages, possibly low Class B

14. Szechwan University, Chengtu

15. Kwangsi University, Liangfang near Kweilin, Kwangsi

16. Fuhtan University, Peipei near Chungking

Unacceptable (plus many others not visited)

17. Cheloo University, Chengtu

18. Hwanan College, Nanping, Fukien
not bad but too small and weak

19. Soochow University, Sinjenmiao near Kukong, Kwangtung
no equipment

20. Kweichow University, Kweiyang, Kweichow

21. Sun Yat-sen University, Pingshih near Kukong, Kwangtung
very bad political situation, no standards, seriously deficient

22. Hangchow University, Shaowu, Fukien
no equipment at all, no faculty, probably closing

23. Canton University, Kukong, Kwangtung
terrible

Memorandum from George B. Cressey
Cultural Relations Program, Chungking

January 2, 1944

SUBJECT Chinese Students Coming to America.

ABSTRACT It appears possible that hundreds, even thousands, of students may shortly come to the United States for technical study. All will be poorly prepared and in need of guidance. Cultural Relations should consider the various problems.

MEMORANDUM

Prospective Arrivals

There is widespread interest in sending Chinese students abroad in large numbers, possibly to a greater extent than ever before. This is partly due to the war-time need for technicians and to the prospective demand for large numbers of trained people in reconstruction. Figures of several thousand are sometimes mentioned, with particular reference to education in America. The desire to go abroad is also intensified by the cheapness of American money at 20 to 1, for students now find it comparatively easy to finance foreign travel. Prices in America appear fantastically cheap in terms of the artificial exchange rate. Some students are also motivated by desire to escape possible military service. It is also true that China is war weary, and educational standards in the universities have become so low that is impossible to secure a good education. Local comments refer to both sending students and factory apprentices.

The interest in going to America is noticeable on every hand, both through articles in the press and in repeated enquiry from students and faculty members. The Central News Agency release for Dec. 30 contains the following item:

327 STUDENTS PASS EXAMINATIONS FOR STUDYING ABROAD

Chungking, Dec. 30 (Central) "Three hundred and twenty seven students have passed the competitive examination for studying abroad held recently under the auspices of the Ministry of Education, according to an official announcement made public today. Altogether 751 students took part in the examination.

Among the successful candidates, 108 will study engineering, 30 science, 7 medicine, 15 agriculture, 74 commerce, 55 law, 28 literature, and 10 education. Majority of the successful candidates are government employees who have been in public service for more than three years."

There is hereafter to be close supervision of all Chinese going abroad, and I find that enrollment in the San Min Chu I Youth Corps has increased as it is reported to facilitate one's permission to go abroad. Prior to departure for

中国赴美留学备忘录（1944）

2

any foreign study, all Chinese must join the Central Training Corps for six weeks and live under spartan military rule. (See separate memorandum dated Jan. 2. While abroad they are to be subject to periodical enquiry as to the correctness of their political views by a representative of the Chinese Ministry of Education. After their return they may again have to go through the Central Training Corps.

Problems

In my talks on American education in wartime I have pointed out that all of our men students and many of our teachers are in government service. Thus many courses have been dropped and graduate study is partially suspended. I have also discreetly endeavored to say that western civilization is a unit and that to borrow science and technology without understanding democracy and philosophy is unwise. This is aimed at the current idea that China should study only science and technology from abroad meanwhile preserving its old social system.

The exchange of students has great possibilities. Under favorable conditions it may be of major value for good will and trade, and in guiding the future internal development of China along lines sympathetic to our way of life. It is certainly desirable for the United States to present its approach to postwar problems alongside the obvious success of Soviet planning. America is now fortunate in that many of the present leaders of China were trained in the United States, and are on the whole sympathetio to us. If this proposed program of sending Chinese students to America reaches the expected proportions we may look forward to another generation of influential friends.

Preparation and Guidance

Almost without exception, these students will be poorly prepared. Both equipment and standards of Chinese universities are quite inferior. Degrees do not mean what they did before the war, and American universities should be cautioned accordingly. The command of English has also deteriorated.

My personal preference would be for almost all of these new arrivals, even though graduates of Chinese universities, to first spend a year as Seniors or even Juniors in small liberal arts colleges prior to undertaking their professional training. And in every case they should be held to very exacting standards. Too often Chinese have received degrees for poor work on the supposition thay they knew more than their poor English indicated. I have even met some who were in the United States for several years who have almost forgotten their English and have gone very far down hill professionally.

Since this new group of students will largely be interested in graduate work, they will gravitate to the larger universities in the larger cities. And as graduate students they will take little part in college life. It would seem desirable that we now plan on much more careful aid to such students than hitherto. This is especially needed for those in utilitarian fields without contacts with the humanities. A broad program of Cultural Relations should supplement the existing agencies such as the churches, Associated Boards for Christian Colleges, International Y.M.C.A., East-West Association, etc.

3

A further danger may arise on the financial side. The present rate of exchange, so temptingly attractive to the Chinese, will probably not continue. Thus many students may find it impossible to meet their expenses and will be in danger of becoming a charge on the American government. Our current generosity to stranded Chinese students is known, and appreciated, and it may be assumed that we would continue to assist those in further difficulty.

Correlary

It is culturally desirable for Chinese students to study in America, it is also worth while for Americans to study in China. Prior to the war there were various preliminary projects of bringing Americans to Yenching or Lingnan for their Junior year. This should be kept in mind for the future, and might even be possible in a small way at present.

Ten Indian students are now here, and ten Chinese students have gone to India.

第三卷

葛德石在中国考察的报告档案

1944年
中国政治及工业考察报告

Memorandum from George B. Cressey
Cultural Relations Program, Chungking

Feb. 8, 1944

SUBJECT Central Land Survey

ABSTRACT This is the principal survey and map printing agency, entirely under the Army. It is located in Kweiyang. The output of maps is large, but the standards are low.

SOURCE OF DATA The Survey was visited on Feb. 2-5, 1944 in company with Major Allan Dotson of the Engineers Corps, attached to General Stilwell's headquarters in New Delhi, who came to China for this purpose. Major Liu of the Chinese Army was also in the party. The visit necessitated a ten day trip by jeep from Kunming to Chungking, as Kweiyang is otherwise inaccessible. Every facility was given by the Survey.

This is believed to be thefirst time that the Survey has been inspected by Americans since its removal from Nanking in 1936. The Survey was also visited by a Col. Blanford (sp?) of the Survey of India last year.

Although many assurances ofcooperation were given, it was not possible to secure any maps in Kweiyang as all releases must be approved by higher authorities in Chungking. Proper negotiations are now under way by the American Army headquarters in Chungking.

SUGGESTED DISTRIBUTION Embassy, FE, RC, Ge, Army Headquarters in Chungking, Military Intelligence Geographic Section Washington, Army Map Service, U. S. Geological Survey attention W. E. Wrather, American Geographical Society of New York

MEMORANDUM

Organization The Central Land Survey is the principal agency for the survey and publication of topographic maps. It is strictly a military organization, the fourth department of the Chinese General Staff. All of its employees are in uniform. The structure is beurocratic and highly restricted.

There are two offices, the Secretariat and the Technological; and three sections, Administrative, Geodetic, and Cartographic. The Survey also operates the Central Land Survey School which is also under the General Staff.

The Survey was organized in Nanking in 1928, with predecessors in Peking dating back to early in the century. The Survey moved to Changsha in 1936, to Kweilin in 1937, and in 1938-40 to Kweiyang and vicinity. A considerable part of the equipment is still in the nearby villages of Changying and Pingpa. The buildings are scattered and very inadequate, more than a dozen in all. Several are mere sheds, one is a converted temple. Most are poor even by Chinese wartime standards.

中央土地调查所备忘录（1944）

Cressey Memo on Central Land Survey 2 Feb. 8, 1944

Personnel The principal officers are as follows.

Lt. General Hsun-pu Yen, Director
Major General Cho-chi Lin Vice Director
Major General Chih-cho Wang Head of Technical Dept. (speaks English)
Major General Tung Chang Head General Affairs Dept.
Major General Wan-hwang Pin Head Second Bureau
Dr. Chien-pai Hsia (recent appointee, rank uncertain)(speaks English)

The Survey is seriously handicapped by the lack of administrative personnel who know foreign languages or understand foreign map standards. The only officials with European training are Drs. Wang and Hsia; no one else speaks English. These two spent a year in England and three years in Germany where they received the Doctor of Engineering degree in 1939. They appear moderately able, but have only been with the Survey for two months. It is expected that General Wang will visit the United States in 1944. The other officers are military men without any indication of sound cartographic understanding, mostly graduates of the training school some thirty years ago.

The total personnel of the Survey now numbers 2,000, including field survey parties. This compares with 6,000 a few years ago. Of the present staff, 130 are qualified in aerial photogrametry but no aerial work is under way. Although all of the 6,000 are members of the army, it is apparently possible for them to resign or secure leaves in order to accept more remunerative pay elsewhere.

Equipment The Survey has a large and expensive array of equipment, now largely in storage. This includes many items probably beyond the skill or needs of the staff.

There is a large array of costly Zeiss Aerotopographic Instruments, some of which are now regarded as obsolete or unsuited for Chinese needs. There are five sets of "Full Automatic Rectifying Apparatus", with five movements. These are large and elaborate instruments of which only one is now set up, this is used only for training purposes. There are also 17 "Multiplex Projectors", with 6 to 9 projectors each. Of these only two are set up, and are used for training only.

The stock of transits, levels and other survey equipment includes the best German, Swiss and English models, with dozens of instruments in storage. There is a 60 x 60 cm. camera in operation, and an 80 z 80 cm. camera in storage. ~~Printing facilit~~

Printing facilities include two old presses for stone lithography plus one which needs repair, and a modern 26 x 28 inch Dresden-Leipziger offset color press, currently used for a six color job. The total electric power available for these presses is a 25 KW generator, frequently out of order. There is said to be another press in Kweilin.

Map Library The Survey is seriously deficient in its Map Library. No count was available, but there are only one to two thousand items outside their own publications. Nor were there foreign books in the field. The only foreign map coverage are very old Japanese sets at 1 / 25,000 and 1 / 50,000 complete. The Libraty apparently even lacks the Survey of India sheets on China. This unfamiliarity with foreign maps and map standards reflects the very limited education and technical competence of those in charge.

The Survey fortunately has a copy of volume two of the Great Soviet World Atlas, and is using its sheets to compile their 1 / 1,000,000 maps of northern Chinese areas.

Cartography At present there are but 40 draftsmen of all grades of ability, whereas the program calls for 144. Most of these draftsmen, and the compilers, appeared to be of low ability, mere pen pushers. One instance was noted of a girl who was drawing in a river along the side of the valley rather than through the contour "v" at the bottom of the slope. Few of the maps showed any feel for geomorphology.

A major technical weakness was the apparent absence of any cartographic theory or mathematical ability.

Survey Coverage The Survey has published between 10,000 and 15,000 maps, almost all of them in one color.

1 / 10,000 Maps at this scale cover the vicinity of Shanghai and Nanking, and are based on aerial photographs. The original negatives are available, and might be of major value for target work.

1 / 20,000 No modern work has been done on this scale, but many maps were made under the Empire prior to 1911.

1 / 25,000 Only a limited number of sheets are available at this scale, chiefly in the vicinity of Nanking, Hankow and Chungking. They are good maps, and modern.

1 / 50,000 This is the major series. To cover all of China, including the outer territories, will require 29,000 sheets. Of these 7,000 are finished of which 1,000 are drawn on Lambert's Conformal Projection with proper grid lines. The publication to date covers almost all of China proper except the northern, western and southern borders of Fukien, northern Shensi, western Kansu, western Szechwan, and the area of the Tsingling Mountains in southern Shensi, southern Kansu and northern Szechwan. Some of the old sheets are compiled rather than surveyed. New editions are available in some areas. Drafting and printing of new sheets is actively under way. One third of the field survey parties are now operating in Sinkiang.

1 / 100,000 This series covers a larger area than the 1/50,000 series, and include all of the provinces except parts of Fukien, and the border provinces of Sinkiang, ~~Chahar,~~ Chinghai, Sikang, etc.

1 / 300,000 Maps on this scale are available for all of China, including Outer Mongolia. Some of the sheets are said to be poor.

Cressey Memo on Central Land Survey 4 Feb. 8, 1944

A new Hankow sheet in colors has just been published, which is said to utilize all astronomic and 1/50,000 data. Preparation of similar maps has been suspended.

1 / 1,000,000 There is said to be an old series covering all of China. New maps are now in preparation conforming to the International series, with 76 sheets projected. Compilation work has been finished for all of the series, and publication could be completed within a year provided that money were available. Due to the current financial inflation, publication may be indefinitely postponed. One-color finished drawings are essentially complete for seven sheets in Outer Mongolia and Northern Manchuria, and 10 others are in the final ink drafting stage. Photographic copies would be supplied, and it is hereby urged that proper requests be made.

Index maps for all of these series are available, by provinces, but the Survey has no map catalogue. The usual printing of the 1/50,000 and 1/100,000 series is 500 copies, and it was noted that the Shansi inventory showed between 300 and 400 copies of each map still on hand. No stocks were lost in the removals from Nanking. Storage is now scattered between Kweiyang, Chungking, Kweilin and elsewhere.

The acquisition of all these maps is of major military value to the United States, especially those at 1/50,000.

Other Maps In addition to the above, the Survey has printed many other maps on the request of the General Staff. Most of these are direct reproductions of foreign maps with Chinese place names added or substituted but usually without credit lines. These include a complete set on Africa at 1/2,000,000 apparently based on the French series, a 2 sheet map of Indo China, a 4 sheet map of the Philippines, a 4 sheet map of Siberia, a 1 sheet map of Malaya, a 4 sheet map of the East Indies, a 12 sheet map of Europe and an 8 sheet map of Asia.

Central Land Survey School The School is directly under the General Staff, but is operated by the Survey. It is at Nanchang, a suburb of Kweiyang. The School moved here in Sept. 194_ from Chengying, nearby, with earlier moves ~~xxxxxx~~ from Nanking to Changsha and Kweilin. It occupies eight large but barren buildings, and has 250 students. Before enteringthe School, students must be Senior High School graduates and take a six months military indoctrination course. All are soldiers, and live under rigorous conditions. The course lasts three years. There are departments for Geodetic Surveying, Topographic Surveying, Aerial Surveying, and Cartography. With minor exceptions, the instructors are army officers. The classrooms visited seemed quite elementary and the standards low.

A total of 754 people have graduated from the course, and 118 more will graduate at the end of February 1944. It is proposed to enlarge the number so that there will be 300 graduates a year. Graduates enter the Survey, and this is the only source of its personnel. Tungchi University also trains surveyors, but they find higher salaries and more attractive positions in other government bureaus. The Survey is thus ingrowing, and

Cressey Memo on Central Land Survey 5 Feb. 8, 1944

is such a closed organization that no new ideas can enter. The present executive officers of the Survey, mostly Generals, are all graduates of the forerunner of this school in Peiping.

Future Plans The Generalissimo has ordered the Survey to complete the mapping of China within ten years after the war. The inadequacy of the present staff is partly appreciated by those in charge, and it is thus proposed to send a number of people abroad, chiefly to the United States. The plans have not yet been approved, but call for ten students to be sent during each of three years, together with a group of apprentices 35, 15 and 10 during each of these three years. The Survey desires advice as to where the students should study, and also as to where the trainees might best be assigned. Supposedly the latter would work with the U. S. Geological Survey, the Army Map Setvice, the Army Engineers, the Air Corps etc.

Evaluation and Problems Like other Chinese organizations, the Survey is to be congratulated on doing work under great difficulties. At the same time there are fundamental weaknesses. Part of these relate to the ultra-secretive and beaurocratic regulations of the Army which regards all map data as confidential and will scarcely release maps to other government organizations.

The major problem of the Survey at present is financial, with salary conditions reported to be but one third those of government universities. Incomes are so low that the staff members are resigning or asking for leaves from which they do not return; apparently the Army is not able to hold its own officers and privates. Draftsmen can secure higher salaries with other government agencies, and so are "on loan". Hence much work is coming to a standstill.

As a result of visits to many factories and institutions, it is clear that China's major war problems are finance and transport. Here is but another example of an agency which could make a much larger contribution to victory if it could solve these two problems.

The low army salary scale and the related problem of securing adequate personnel is illustrated in the case of Dr. Chih-cho Wang, who came to the Survey two months ago from the China Institute of Geography, together with Dr. Chien-pai Hsia. Dr. Wang received his doctorate in 1939 and is both young and without major experience, though pleasant and probably with a future. In order to provide an adequate salary, he was given the rank of Major General.

An important shortcoming is the absence of broad minded and professionally competent leadership, with international standards of scholarship. Nowhere down the line did I find adequate ability. The necessary technical literature does not exist in Chinese, yet very few of the staff read any foreign language.

The Survey would genuinly welcome an American cartographer or surveyor. Such a person might be supplied by the Department of State's program of Technical Experts, possibly on loan from the Geological Survey; or by someone from the U. S. Army. This is the psychological moment for the United States to guide a fundamental program.

Cressey Memo on Central Land Survey 6 Feb. 8, 1944

The Survey needs samples of what maps may be like. It would appear to be a wise policy for the Army Map Service, the Geological Survey, and the American Geographical Society to donate large collections of maps.

When General Wang and others visit the United States, they should receive an official welcome and adequate introductions.

A further problem lies in the failure of the General Staff to realize the importance of a map program, both through adequate support and standards. Extreme restrictions are placed on the release of maps. I was told in confidence that a former director was severely reprimanded for giving certain maps to the Survey of India without authorization.

The cartographic program of the National Geological Survey stands in striking contrast, for the latter has high standards of scholarship, competent personnel, and a map library of 40,000 items. It would seem desirable for China to reorganize its map service under civilian direction.

Other Chinese Map Sources In my airgram of Dec. 27, 1943, I referred to the extensive unpublished collection of topographic maps at the Chinese Geological Survey in Peipei, near Chungking. This especially refers to drawings at 1 / 500,000.

I have also found excellent unpublished maps on Sinkiang on a scale of 1 / 500,000. These are being drwan by Professor P. L. Yuan of the Department of Geolo y at the National Southwest Associated University in Kunming. Prof. Yuan spent five years in the northwest with Sven Hedin, and the maps are especially valuable for their road information. The maps use Chinese names for places, rather than the Mongol names as used on Soviet maps. The series is entitled "Sinkiang Province and Adjacent Regions", and the drawings are beautiful three color jobs, with topography in shading. The series will contain 42 maps, of which 6 in the Altai Mountain area are complete, and 9 in the Tien Shan nearly finished.

I have introduced Major Dotson to both the Geological Survey and to Professor Yuan, and have strongly urged that the drawings be flown to India in order to be photographed for the Army Map Service. Both parties are willing to make their material available provided that the Chinese Army authorities make no objection.

Chinese Maps to America In view of the basic importance of map information, it appears highly desirable that the United States acquire complete coverage for China, at all scales. I have urged the American Army headquarters in Chungking to secure sets of all of these maps, not only for the Army Map Service and theatre operations, but also for the Office of the Geographer of the Department of State and for the American Geographical Society in New York.

G.B.C.

Memorandum from George B. Cressey
Cultural Relations Program, Chungking

Jan. 2, 1944

SUBJECT Central Training Corps

ABSTRACT The Central Training Corps is a party program by which to indoctrinate all government officials. It operates along strict military lines and includes much good information but with fascist tendencies. All those going abroad must attend.

SUGGESTED DISTRIBUTION Embassy, RC, FE, etc.

MEMORANDUM

I visited the Central Training Corps on Dec. 6 upon the invitation of Lt. Gen. Wong Tung-yuen, as arranged by my friend and geographical colleague Professor K. C. Huang. After inspecting the large and excellent plant and having tea, I spoke to the 800 trainees on "America at War". I understand that I am to be invited for dinner by General Wang.

The Central Training Corps is one of the favorite projects of the Generalissimo. He speaks at the Memorial Service each Sunday without fail, discussing citizenship and China's problems. The Corps is a party rather than a government project, but is staffed by Army officers. It is run on spartan military lines. The trainees wear plain army uniforms, live in simple barracks, and eat very plain food.

The program usually lasts six weeks, although some periods are shorter, and the groups usually number 400 to 500. The current class is the 28th, so that the Corps has been operating for several years. Early in 1944 an advanced six months program is to be added.

This is a very important training and indoctrination school, designed "to familiarize the peoplewith the party organization." The classes once included army officers, but now are largely made up of civilians. These range from division chiefs to vice ministers, with many college professors and even college presidents. Attendance is usually compulsory, but a few volunteer and must be passed by a Board. If one is ordered to attend, exemption is granted only for one of ten reasons. These include physical weakness, over 50 years in age, currently out of the country, at the front, essential in present position, disease (including piles!). The excuse of being too busy is not accepted. However a select few are able to satisfy the requirements by merely attending five evenings during each of three classes; such people are called directors.

The program is very strenuous, with rigorous military drill, rifle practice, and long hours. It is reported that some would almost rather give up their position than attend. During part of the day the "students" listen to lectures on government organization, the work of various ministries, the war and reconstruction, San Min Chu I, hsien organization, and party plans. Considerable literature is distributed.

中央训练团备忘录（1944）

Cressey Memo on Central Training Corps 2 Jan. 2, 1944

Before leaving the Corps it is almost essential to join the party, and I have only learned of two who successfully refused. Various political advantages accrue to those who graduate. At the end of the program the trainees receive a certificate and a signed picture of the Generalissimo. The alumni must make frequent reports. I also have been told that their promotion or demotion, and shift to other positions is also involved, but I have no direct reports of the misuse of this power.

Among those in the current class afe 72 who shortly plan to go abroad. Hereafter all students and officials without exception must attend before leaving the country. It is also reported but not confirmed that a further period of indoctrination must follow their return. I was not able to find out that this preparatory training involved instructions as to taking pictures or collecting information of possible military value as may have been true in pre-war Japan.

Since visiting the Corps I have heard a good deal about it from various Chinese friends. Almost no one had any enthusiasm for the program, although it is recognized as a useful unifying factor and it offers opportunity for personal contact with the Generalissimo. University people certainly find it an inconvenience, and far too strenuous for their present physical condition.

China certainly needs intelligent coherence, but this party program appears too dangerously fascist and anti-democratic. Several people have commented on the Corps as an indication of the extent to which German ideas still dominate. It will be remembered that German military officials remained in China during the early years of the Sino-Japanese war.

Memorandum from George B. Cressey
Cultural Relations Program, Chungking

June 6, 1944

SUBJECT Central Political Institute

ABSTRACT The Institute is the agency of the Party for training civil officials. It is located in the country south of Chungking, and has 2,000 students.

SOURCE OF DATA The Institute was visited on June 5, 1944.

SUGGESTED DISTRIBUTION Embassy, FE, SEA, etc.

Memorandum

The Central Political Institute is under the Kuomintang, rather than the Ministry of Education, but its academic standards are said to be comparable with the universities. It exists to prepare civil servants for national, provincial and local government, with varying emphasis from year to year according to the need. Many of the current graduates become hsien officials.

The Institute was founded in Nanking in 1927, where it had some 500 students. During the war it moved to Kuling, then to Hunan, and in 1938 to an attractive site near the South Hot Springs, half an hour by car south of Chungking.

There are three divisions. 1. Civil Service Training, with a four months program for those who have passed the Civil Service examinations. These people are all college graduates, and currently number 400. 2. The Collegiate Section offers a four year program to approximately 1400 students, all of them Middle School graduates. There are five departments, namely Administration and Law, Diplomacy (here the ability in English is greater than in other departments), Economics, Journalism, and Land Administration. 3. Technical Training, a two year program for 300 Middle School graduates. The total registration is 2050, of whom about 50 are girls. There is no current Senior class as no Freshmen were admitted in 1939 or 1940 due to war conditions.

In addition there is the Post-Graduate School of Journalism in Chungking, a Research Bureau with no students, and a Graduate Division.

The teaching staff numbers 120, one fifth of whom have outside jobs due to the high costs of living. Professors number 64, including some 50 returned students. Forty six army officers are employed by the Institute, at army rates of pay, for training, to maintain discipline, and to supervise the daily life of the students.

Party instruction is provided in about the same extent as with the universities, namely San Min Chu I for Freshmen, but party functions and party activities are much more emphasized. There is much attention to military discipline. Thus all students wear a uniform, in army style. Discipline is stressed not so much as a stimulus to national loyalty

中央政治研究所备忘录（1944）

Cressey Memo on Central Political Institute 2 June 6, 1944

and patriotism, but "to achieve unity and a new mode of life", or as otherwise stated "regimentation is needed in order to create teamwork." The students seemed somewhat less able and alert than at the better universities. Upon graduation, students must accept whatever government position is assigned to them. They may resign only if permitted by their superior officer.

All expenses of the students are provided, including full tuition, room, board, and clothes. It was reported elsewhere that the Central Political Institute has a larger budget than any of the Ministry of Education institutions.

The extensive campus lies in a small valley beside a reservoir. Many trees were planted upon arrival and have now grown sufficiently to give an attractive atmosphere. Everything is neat and orderly, but there is no apparent plan to the campus. A new auditorium seating 2,000 and built by contributions from the alumni has just been opened. It is probably the finest structure of its kind in Free China.

The Chancellor is General Chiang Kai-shih, while the acting head is Vice Chancellor Cheng Tien-fong. The address is South Hot Springs, Chungking.

NATIONAL LIBRARY OF PEIPING

REPORT FOR 1943

This report covers the work of the Library for the year ending December 1943. It deals with the most eventful period in the history of the Library. Internally the headlong inflation created and continues to create new and urgent problems always waiting for solution. It not only caused a considerable shift in staff personnel, but it also forced us to abandon many of our activities which would have been useful to China's war effort. Internationally our effort to establish closer contact with the outside world has not had as much a success as we had anticipated. Difficulties of transportation has been partially responsible for this failure, but the lack of foreign exchange crippled us to such an extent that our contact even with India was cut to a minimum. Many useful books and scientific journals from India could be transported by air to China, if we only have had the necessary funds.

For financial reasons, therefore, we have to concentrate our efforts to certain limited fields. The following report sketches the major fields of concentration for the year under review.

ACQUISITION OF SOURCE MATERIALS

(1) Lolo Manuscripts. In the spring of this year, our attention was called to the possibility of acquiring a unique collection of Lolo manuscripts which had been preserved in the family of the chieftain of a local tribe adjouring Wuting, Yunnan. A member of our staff was sent to Wuting in June for the purpose of examining and evaluating these manuscripts. With the primitive communication in that almost inaccessible region, it took seven days by horse from Kunming to the home of the owner. However, the price asked for was so prohibitive that the negotiations for its purchase lasted for several months. It was not until the middle of November that the owner agreed to sell the manuscripts en bloc. With a special grant of $100,000 from the Ministry of Education and with personal assistance from Mr. S.L. Ma, an expert of Lolo language, the whole collection of 509 volumes of Lolo manuscripts, 14 volumes of Lolo printed books and 12 volumes of Chinese official records were acquired. In addition, the owner presented to the Library 15 pieces of wooden blocks carved with Lolo characters. These manuscripts and books were carried to Kunming by horse and by chair and delivered to our Kunming office by a Lolo messenger sent by the chieftain of the local tribe.

These manuscripts, dating back from the Ming Dynasty, are the earliest manuscripts in existance and are considered as "classics" in Lolo literature. The collection is not only the largest one in the world, but it forms the most valuable source material from the linguistic and historical point of view. Such a collection of Lolo literature, now made available

北平图书馆报告（1944）

in the Library, will furnish to scholars a mine of information concerning the history and culture of the Lolo tribes hitherto concentrated in Southwestern China. If systematically studied, these manuscripts will greatly facilitate the further exploration of a new scientific field.

(2) Moso Manuscripts. In our previous report mention was made of a collection of Moso manuscripts which had been built up by the Library during the years 1941 and 1942. Continued efforts have been made to acquire more manuscripts as they become available in the market. Moso language is closely related with Tibetan and it possesses two systems of writing, one hieroglyphic and the other syllabic, both different from the Tibetan writing which is derived from the devanagari form of the Hindu alphabet. A considerable amount of literature, mostly of religious significance, in either form of writing, is available only in manuscript form. The only place, however, for their acquisition is Likiang, a remote district north of Tali, Yunnan. It is, therefore, necessary that a member of our staff should remain there in order not to miss any important manuscript whenever it is available. Over 4,000 manuscripts have so far been acquired which will take several years for scholars to work on.

(3) Current Chinese Serial Publications. For the year of 1943, the book fund granted by the China Foundation amounted only to CN$30,000 which amount is barely enough to cover our subscriptions to current serial publications, leaving very little money for the purchase of Chinese books. More money is urgently needed for current and perishable materials especially in view of the fact that they are printed in limited editions in wartime. Unless they are acquired immediately after their publication, they become easily out of print.

(4) Western Books from India. Under a grant of US$1,000 from the China Foundation, 350 volumes of western books were bought in India last April. Several Indian scientific institutions contributed to the Library a number of books, pamphlets and journals. They were packed in one wooden box and seven large bundles and sent by air from Calcutta to Kunming through the assistance of the China-Burma Transport Administration. All of these books were received early in August in perfect condition.

While in India, the undersigned was able to expedite the dispatch of 61 cases of books and scientific instruments ordered from the United States by the Ministry of Education for the use of Chinese universities. These cases have been stored over a year in several godowns at Karachi awaiting for transportation. From Karachi they were first sent by rail to Calcutta and shipped from there by steamer to Dibrugarh. They were transported from Dibrugarh by air to Kunming. From July to October, 61 cases of books and scientific instruments were received in this way. Our Kunming office was ordered by the Ministry of Education to redistribute them to various colleges and universities at the expense of the ministry.

(5) Subscription to American Journals. Through a grant of US$600 from the China Foundation, the subscription to American journals has been kept up-to-date. The work of ordering,

- 3 -

checking and storing of these periodicals at the University of Rochester was undertaken by the Committee on Aid to Libraries in War Areas of the American Library Association. Our grateful acknowledgments are due to Mr. John R. Russell, Chairman of the Committee and to Mr. Roger S. Greene, Vice-Director of the China Foundation, who made all the necessary contacts on behalf of the Library. As more American and British journals are needed by the Library, the China Foundation has been urged to make larger appropriations on periodical subscriptions to meet the future needs of Chinese scholars.

(6) Japanese and Puppet Governments' materials. The work of collecting Japanese and Puppet Governments' materials has been continued in occupied areas in spite of financial and other difficulties. All of these materials have been stored in safe places in Shanghai and will be made available as soon as peace is restored. While China and other United Nations are concentrating their efforts on defeating Japan, it would be a folly to neglect the large and revealing literature which the Japanese themselves have reproduced. Outside of Japan, the only possible place for collecting and storing such material is Shanghai. In view of the importance of continuing the present collection specially built up for the use of scholars in the future, it is hoped that further financial support could be secured from friends of the Library.

EDITORIAL WORK

With a reduced staff, it has not been possible to continue much of the editorial work initiated in preceeding years. However, the following projects are either nearing completion or partially completed:

(1) Annotated Bibliography relating to Sinkiang. This useful bibliography has been compiled by Mr. Wan Sze-nien and consists of four main sections arranged by languages: (1) Chinese, (2) Japanese; (3) English and French and (4) Russian. It includes books and periodical articles concerning Sinkiang published up to 1937. In view of its important political and economic position, such a systematic bibliography will be found most useful to scholars and administrators. It will be published as soon as financial support is secured.

(2) Who's Who of American Returned Students. In the present war of resistance against Japan, the American returned students are playing a very important part. They will, no doubt, exert much influence on post-war reconstruction. In cooperation with the Chinese-American Institute of Cultural Relations, a Who's Who (in English) is now being compiled. It aims to be a fairly complete survey of trained personnel returned from the United States. It is hoped that the publication of this survey will be a contribution to the organization of personnel in China.

(3) Who's Who of British Returned Students. In cooperation with the Sino-British Cultural Association, a Who's Who of British Returned Students (in English) has been compiled. This directory gives a fairly complete survey of all those who have studied in British universities and would serve as a useful book of reference in the field of biographical literature.

- 4 -

(4) Directory of Organizations in China Concerned with the United States. With a view to locating the principal American agencies in China which have active programs concerned with this country and the Chinese agencies which are affiliated with American institutions, a Directory of Organizations in China Concerned with the United States (In English) will be compiled. In addition to their names and addresses, the nature of their organization and the scope of their activities will be included. It will be similar in scope to the Directory of Organizations in America concerned with China, compiled by Wilma Fairbank and published by the American Council of Learned Societies. Such a directory has long been felt as it has frequently been requested by both Chinese and Americans who are interested in the promotion of Sino-American cultural relations.

REPUBLICATION OF THE QUARTERLY BULLETIN

With a grant from the Ministry of Education, the Library was able to resume the publication of the Quarterly Bulletin of Chinese Bibliography suspended since the outbreak of the Pacific War. Owing to shortage of paper and difficulties of printing, it was decided to issue combined numbers for the duration of the war. Of the Chinese edition, the joint issue for March-June was published in July and was very well received by the scholarly world. The joint issue for September-December is now in press and will be published in January, 1944. Two thousand copies of each issue are printed and distributed.

In cooperation with the Chinese-American Institute of Cultural Relations, the English edition of the Bulletin resumed its publication beginning from its New Series Volume 3. The joint issue for March-June was published in September and a sample copy was sent by air by the American Embassy to Washington. In October it was reproduced by photo offset process by the American Council of Learned Societies. From a recent cable from Washington, it was learned that 400 copies of the Bulletin were reproduced and were received with interest by American scholars.

Despite the difficulties of printing and publishing in Free China, there is a remarkable output of current literature of which Western scholars are as yet totally unaware. This Bulletin is the only medium through which this increasing volume of Chinese literature is recorded and reviewed and should be a most useful aid to all scholars.

REFERENCE WORK AND OTHER SERVICES

The continuance of the war has put increasing pressure on the Library to undertake certain immediate services. First, it has to meet heavy demand for consultative aid and information, as it was often called upon to supply with essential data about the war in Europe, war-time legislation, problems of post-war reconstruction, about bibliographical sources and about expert personnel. With a reduced staff, we had to adapt our program to these emergency needs and our staff members gave freely of their time in furnishing background material to all those who requested them.

- 5 -

Secondly, the work of supplying latest information about the scientific achievements of the west has been greatly facilitated by the regular supply of microfilms from the Department of State at Washington. In view of the importance of the material contained therein, one member of our staff is devoting his whole time in reading over the films and in recording the most important scientific inventions and discoveries. Three members of our staff have been transferred to the International Cultural Service of China to assist in the development of its microfilm program.

Thirdly, linked with the microfilm program, but serving a specific purpose, is the monthly publication in English of the Reference Series issued since January of this year. In each issue there were reproduced in memeographed form important diplomatic documents concluded among foreign governments since the outbreak of the Pacific War. It was an attempt at wider dissemination of information about the West and our effort was very much appreciated by government agencies and individuals scholars who are engaged in the study of international affairs. While there was an urgent demand for source material of this kind, our financial difficulties forced us to suspend its publication in August until further support could be secured.

Fourthly, with a view to assisting Chinese and foreign libraries in the acquisition of Chinese materials published in wartime, the Library lent its financial and other assistnace to the Chinese Library Association under whose auspices a Chinese Book Service has recently been organized. A trained member of our staff was transferred to the Association to assist in this program. In answer to a cable inquiry from the American Library Association, the undersigned made proposals for joint cooperative acquisitions of Chinese material by American libraries. The Association also undertakes to store them for American libraries for the duration of the war. The successful execution of this project would avoid unnecessary duplication of labor and would in the long run be a measure of economy.

STAFF CHANGES

The steeply rising cost of living has hit our staff very hard. Neither the rice allowance of the Government nor the special cost-of-living subsidies avail to provide them with a moderate standard of comfort. In the course of one year, no less than 12 members of our staff have resigned in order to accept better paid positions elsewhere. In view of the scarcity of trained personnel, it is necessary that the salaries of our staff be increased, so that they can support their families with a higher standard of living without worrying too much about the daily necessities of life. As our staff has now been reduced to 26, it has not been possible to render useful services ~~as much~~ as we wished. Looking ahead to the immeidate post-war period, it is hoped that our staff may be strengthened in order to prepare ourselves for the greater task of post-war rehabilitation and reconstruction.

Respectfully submitted,

T. L. Yuan
Director

December 31, 1943

Memorandum from George B. Cressey
Cultural Relations Program, Chungking

Jan. 11, 1944

SUBJECT Chikiang Electro-Chemical Metallurgical Works

ABSTRACT This new National Resources Commission plant produces sponge iron, open hearth steel, electric furnace steel alloys, steel castings, rolled sheets and forms to 16 inches, electrolytic copper, zinc, and refractory brick.

SOURCE OF DATA The plant was visited on Jan. 8 and 9, 1944 through the kindness of Dr. Wong Wen-hao, head of the National Resources Commission. The party included Mr. Trone consultant to T.V. Soong, J.A. Keane of United States Steel Export, James Penfield of the Chungking Embassy, Joseph Needham of the Sino-British Scientific Mission, and Messrs. W.W. Kintner, Macmillan, and George B. Cressey of the Cultural Relations Program. The party was housed in the guest house and given every facility by the manager, Mr. C.P. Yap.

SUGGESTED DISTRIBUTION Embassy, Chungking Lend-Lease, RC, Ge, Washington agencies concerned such as Military Intelligence, OEW, OSS.

MEMORANDUM

Plant Description The Chikiang Electro-Chemical Metallurgical Works is 120 km. by road south of Chungking, of which 100 km. is on the main road to Kweiyang and 20 km. on the road east to Hunan which branches near the village of Chikiang. The plant is actually at Sanche (three streams) where the Sungkan Ho and the Pu Ho unite to form the Chi Kiang, a tributary of the Yangtze. The country is hilly to sub-mountainous, with almost no level land. The Chin Kiang is navigable for medium size junks, and navigation is improved by half a dozen 25 foot dams with locks measuring some 100 by 20 feet. Smaller boats can continue up each tributary stream above Sanche.

This is a National Resources Commission enterprise, one of a hundred, and dates from 1940. It is directed by Mr. Yap Chu-phay (Yeh Chu-p'ei), an Amoy Chinese who has spent many years in America as a consulting engineer. While in New York City he earned $10,000 a year, while now he receives $80 a month, due to inflation. He has boundless energy, great resourcefulness, and wide competence. The engineering design is excellent and everything is ship-shape.

There are 1400 employees, plus 206 on the staff of whom 40 are returned students.

The laboratories are well equipped, and staffed by scientists who appear to understand fundamentals. The metallographic equipment includes an xray machine and microscopes.

綦江电化冶炼厂备忘录（1944）

-2-

The plant location is determined by the junction of the two streams down which come coal and iron, and the intersection of the highway. There is water connection with the Yangtze. The local raw materials are of inferior quality, so that the plant probably has no post war future. Its great value is as a war-time source of supply and as a training school for engineers and skilled workers.

This is one of the numerous cases where Chinese technicians have created a thoroughly modern plant with only a few lathes and similar tools, plus electric equipment. The machinery and installation is all of local design and construction from the ground up. Many novel improvisations are necessary but the result is a finished job which will meet engineering standards anywhere. Production is microscopic by American standards, but the quality is good. Chikiang is an excellent demonstration that Chinese can master technical skills.

Products The installations and products are as follows.

1. Sponge iron, from a novel rotary kiln producing 10 tons a day.
2. Open Hearth steel ingots, with foundry for castings. Also high carbon tool steel.
3. Rolling mill, 16 inch, four stands, two high, ready by Spring.
4. Electric high frequency furnace for alloy steels such as aluminum, nickel, chromium; also silol, nicro-silol, nickel hard, and duriron.
5. Copper convertor, melting old cash
6. Electrolytic copper, with a plant capacity of 3 tons daily, shortly to be doubled.
7. Zinc roasting plant and facilities from obtaining zinc from old coins. Also electrolytic zinc, zinc oxide, and zinc sulphate.
8. Bronze castings
9. Refractory brick, such as fire brick, insolation, dolomite, magnesite, and silica brick.

Sponge Iron Sponge iron is produced in a kiln of local design which somewhat resembles a double cement kiln. The cylinders are 8 feet in diameter, with an upper inclined pre-heat chamber 40 feet long, a lower 80 foot combustion chamber, and 20 foot precombustion cylinder. Powdered coke or charcoal and 8 mesh ore are fed into the top cyclinder, and producer gas at the lower end. The advantage lies in the utilization of low grade high ash coal, since local coke is poor and inadequate. The product is a coarse powder. It will be used in the open hearth plant, and as a melt in the electric furnaces to facilitate melting of scrap.

The capacity is ten tons a day, but operations are not yet satisfactory. The iron ore averages 40 to 42 per cent fe. The reaction is Fe_2O_3 to Fe_3O_4 to FeO to Fe.

-3-

Ore comes from 40 km. up the Pu Ho at Kanshui. Coal is mined up the Pu Ho at Nantung; it is of Permian age and carries 3 per cent sulphur, so that low sulphur Jurassic coal is brought from a distance.

Open Hearth The Open Hearth furnace appears to be of unusually good design, better than many old furnaces in the United States. It is housed in a modern reinforced concrete and brick structure with efficient lay out. The furnace is still in construction but should be in operation in February. The capacity is 15 to 18 tons per heat, with 2 to 3 heats a day. This will be the largest open hearth furnace in China, comparing with the 8 to 10 ton furnace at Tatoukou and the 8 to 10 furnace of the China Development Company, both built from designs 40 years old.

White pig iron from native blast furnaces elsewhere will be used, plus local sponge iron. The stockpile of the former amounts to 1000 tons, valued at $20,000,000 CNC.

There is both an old and a new foundry, with skilled workers. It is even proposed to cast steel rails and bomb casings.

Steam forging facilities include one 1 ton and two ½ ton hammers.

Rolling Mill Rolling mills are the major steel bottleneck in China. Only the 24th Arsenal has a mill in operation. (see the Memorandum on Tse Yu Steel dated Jan. 11)

This mill should be in operation in 3 to 4 months, as most of the material is ready. It is a 16 inch four stand two high installation. Design and construction are local, including chilled rollers. It will produce narrow sheets and plates (some for small oil drums for the Kansu fields), angle iron, I beams to 4 inches, and silicon sheet. Power will come from a 500 HP marine motor, rebuilt from an old steamer.

Electric Steel There are two 1000 ton and two 300 ton high frequency Ajax Northrup furnaces. These are in operation, and produce alloy tool steels with al, ni and cr. There is no tungsten and a few hundred pounds would go a long way.

Copper Old copper cash of wide variety in composition are melted in a special blast furnace, and there is also a reverbatory furnace for refining. The electrolytic cell plant has a capacity of 3 tons a day, and the installation of duplicate equipment is nearly complete. Full operation is seldom possible due to the shortage of furnace copper.

There are casting facilities for bronze.

-4-

The plant has 500 tons of old coins on hand, and expects more. Very large shipments were made to Japan a decade ago, but supplies are still available in the interior.

China's actual copper production is said to be about 1000 tons a year, of which half goes into electric wire and half to the arsenals. Two other electrolytic copper plants are in Kunming and Chungking, each reported to have a capacity of 3 tons a day.

ZINC Zinc is extracted from the coins, and possibly also from Hunan ore.

Refractory Brick Much attention has been given to producing furnace brick of high quality. Local fire clays are available. Production includes fire, insolation, dolomite, magnesite and silica brick. Natural sandstone bricks, quarried to size, are also used.

Memorandum from George B. Cressey
Cultural Relations Program, Chungking

Feb. 11, 1944

SUBJECT Kunming Copper Refinery

ABSTRACT This modern plant produces copper, zinc and aluminum, but is not operating at capacity since the Arsenals can secure cheaper metals through Lend-lease.

SOURCE OF DATA The plant was visited on January 19 with J. Marshall Morris of F.E.A. through the courtesy of the National Resources Commission.

SUGGESTED DISTRIBUTION Embassy, FE, RC, Ge, FEA Chungking; Washington agencies such as Military Intelligence, O.S.S., O.E.W. and Bureau of Mines.

Memorandum

Organization The Kunming Copper Refinery is one of several large industries in the western outskirts of Kunming. It secures electricity from the Lakeside Electric Works and supplies electrolytic copper to the Central Electric Works next door.

The refinery has but 3 dynamos, 1 each devoted to copper, zinc and aluminum. Any increase in production of 1 metal would necessitate shutting down on another.

There is a staff of 30 and 300 workmen. The plant design is modern and operation is satisfactory.

Copper The bulk of the copper is obtained from the Tungchwan mines in northern Yunnan with small supplies from Hunan. Only minor amounts are derived from melted coin. Tungchwan is the leading copper producer in China. Its product must be shipped by mule back so that it is impossible for them to make 100 kilogram annodes. Instead they ship small ingots of blister copper which must be remelted locally. This has a composition of 90-98% copper. The refinery produces copper of 99.93% purity. The local production is melted in two reverbatory furnaces which have a capacity of 4 tons of wire bars a day. Ninety per cent of the product goes into wire.

Output during recent years has been as follows: 1941, 299 tons; 1942, 209 tons; 1943, 312 tons. Since the potential capacity is 4 tons a day, or 1500 tons a year, it is obvious that the refinery is not used to the full. This is said to be due to the lack of an adequate market for costs are so high that many customers cannot afford the necessary price. In reality it is related to the lower cost of Lend-lease copper which is flown in by the United States and supplied to the arsenals at a nominal rate.

昆明炼铜厂备忘录（1944）

The total copper production in China both from ore and coins is estimated to be 1,000 tons a year. Lend-lease supplies are in addition.

The electrolytic mud yields 1% silver and a small amount of gold.

The production at the Tungchwan mine in northern Yunnan is now 1 ton per day, and has never exceeded 30 tons per month, as compared with an estimated capacity of 3 tons. Due to the increasing cost of transportation, the shortage of coal, inadequate manpower and the need for more electricity, the output is shortly to be lowered to one-half ton per day. The mine manager reports that if all these were remedied production might theoretically reach 10 tons per day, but this appears doubtful without improved transportation. At Tungchwan the metallic copper already blocked out equals 200,000 tons with an additional 1,200,000 tons of probable copper. The entire ore body averages 4.2% copper. There are 40,000 tons of old reject ore on the surface which averages 4% copper which might be recovered by improved methods.

Zinc The refinery produced 41 tons of zinc in 1943. There is a capacity of 6 tons per month, installed at the request of the Ministry of War who then refused to buy the products since zinc can be obtained easier through Lend-lease.

Of the 80 tons of zinc ore utilized to date, 20 have come from Tungchwan; 40 from Hunan and 20 from Hweili in southern Sikang. The production of zinc ore from Sikang amounting to 30 tons per month now moves to Chungking for refining.

There are said to be large post-war zinc possibilities in the Kochiu tin area of southern Yunnan with nearby coal and hydroelectricity. There is no production in this area at present.

Aluminum Large deposits of high grade bauxite have recently been discovered in Yunnan and Kweichow; and the refinery has installed an experimental pilot plant. This uses a combination of the Deville and Bayer processes for making Al_2O_3. For the final reduction there is a bank of 5 furnaces, each with 8 electrodes, and a capacity of 6 to 12 kilograms per furnace per day. Experimental production started in October 1943. There is a capacity of 2 tons per month which will be increased to 3 tons a month at the end of 1944, provided electric power is available. The actual production to date is 1 ton of Al_2O_3 and 10 kilograms of aluminum. The former shortage of cryolite has been remedied.

The bauxite deposits at Tsaopu village 43 kilometers west of Kunming were also visited. Bauxite of excellent quality occurs over an area of several square miles. At the surface it is typical pisolitic ore; yellow, brown and red. This grades into dense grey colodial ore with higher silica below the

-3-

surface. Since no pits have yet been dug, the relation of the pisolitic ore to the grey collodial proto-bauxite is not clear. This grey ore contains 40 to 50% $Al_2O_3$and considerable silica, and may require special treatment. The ore is carboniferous in age with limestone above and below. In some instances the grey ore occurs as lenses within the limestone up to 50 meters thick. Similar bauxite is present at Makaitze near the refinery, at Wenchuan (hot springs) at Tapuche, and also in Kweichow where the grey colloidal ore predominates. The composition is as follows:

	Tsaopu	Wenchuan
SiO_2	5.58 %	2.95
Al_2O_3	66.65	64.16
Fe_2O_2	11.92	15.69
TiO_2	3.23	3.00

Memorandum from George B. Cressey
Cultural Relations Program, Chungking

Feb. 14, 1944.

SUBJECT <u>Central Machine Works</u>

ABSTRACT This is the largest machine works in China; a part of the National Resources Commission and located near Kunming. The elaborate equipment includes a million dollars(US)worth of lathes etc. There are seven factories for foundry work, boilers, internal combustion engines, large electrical machinery, machine tools, textile machines, and miscellaneous work.

SOURCE OF DATA The plant was visited on January 22 in company with an M. Robert Rutherford of the American Consulate, through the courtesy of the National Resources Commission.

SUGGESTED DISTRIBUTION Embassy, FE? RC? Ge, FEA Chungking, Washington agencies such as Military Intelligence, OSS, OEW and Bureau of Mines

MEMORANDUM

<u>Description</u> The Central Machine Works is the largest plant of its kind in China. It is under the National Resources Commission and has been intensely developed since the outbreak of the war. It was started in Hunan in 1937, but moved to Yunnan in 1938. Most of the equipment was brought in over the Indo-China Railway five years ago, but some arrived later over the Burma Road. The equipment then cost between three and four million Chinese dollars, probably equal to US$1,000,000. Two-thirds of it is Americ an and one-third German. Due to inflation the capital value is now reported to be CNC$1,400,000,000.

There is a staff of 500 and 1,700 workers. Many of these are young boys. The apprentices school has a considerable number of 13 year old boys and all apprentices are under 18. It seemed strange to find such elaborate and costly equipment operated by very young workers.

It is planned to send a number of college graduate apprentices to America for Training.

The site is in a valley amid the hills and was chosen for security reasons, including the possibility of digging tunnels for air raid safety. Much of the best equipment is housed in a dozen shelters.

<u>Organization</u> The works is organized in seven factories, as follows:

中央机器厂备忘录（1944）

.2.

1. Foundary and steel manufacturing, with a large foundry floor and adequate pattern shop. There is a two ton and five ton cupalo. Steel comes entirely from the Yunnan Iron and Steel Works at Anning. There are three pneumatic hammers one of 300 kilos and two of 50 kilos. Hydraulic presses are of 300 and 400 tons capacity.

2. Boilers and accessories, including condensers. Some plate is on hand. There are rollers for bending boiler plate up to ½ inch.

3. Internal combustion engines, to 220 H.P. for gas and 150 H.P. for oil. Five of the former have been made.

4. Electrical machinery includes large alternators, in comparison with the smaller items produced by the Central Electric Works.

5. Machine tools include lathes, planers and numerous small items such as micrometers. The equipment for this work is particularly elaborate and includes very complicated machines which give the impression of being beyond the apparent needs.

6. Textile machinery.

7. Miscellaneous products, such as microscope stands for the optical factory of the Peiping Academy who themselves manufacture the lenses. Five hundred microscopes have now been built.

Supplies Electric power comes from the Lakeside Works; none is produced locally.

Steel is from Anning, plus some plate still on hand.

Copper is obtained from Tungchwan and the 98 percent purity is adequate.

Scrap Aluminum is shipped to the United States from American planes which have crashed. No Japanese planes are so used. Eight tons were melted in January.

The major shortages are high speed steel, grinding wheels, and condenser tubes. Transportation is also a bottleneck.

Evaluation This is the outstanding machine plant in China, with by far the most complex machinery. It gave a little impression of being a fancy toy for which some bright returned student ordered equipment from pretty pictures in a catalogue.

The production in 1943 exceeded that in 1942, but is still not up to capacity. This is inevitable as the Works operates on miscellaneous orders as received, rather than concentrating on a line of specialized products for which there may be no market.

.3.

The products are shipped as far as Chungking and Sian, but not eastward where older pre-war plants are available.

There is no direct war production, though the products are indirectly valuable. The ~~worker~~ market problem is shown by the fact that there are on hand two dozen drill presses and the same number of pumps for which there is no customer.

1944年
葛德石致中国人民书（英文版）

Written by George B. Cressey
Syracuse University (for free circulation but not for publication)

A LETTER TO CHINA

From An American Friend

These are important days for China, the most significant since the Revolution. Never have the opportunities been greater, nor the possibilities more serious. If we take the right track the future is bright and China may emerge as one of the leading world powers; if we fail the consequences will affect the whole world. I alternately thrill and despair. We surely need intelligence and courage, as well as perspective.

I should like to write as a sincere friend of China, and because I want you to think about what I say rather than who I am, I leave this letter unsigned. I have known China for many years and within recent months I have travelled through nine provinces. Instead of listing all the fine things which might be said or criticizing the shortcomings, I should like to analyze the problems and suggest possible solutions. And though I write as an American, I am also part of China. The world is now so small and so interdependent that what happens here influences all the rest of us. Some of these ideas are my own, but many have come from talking with hundreds of people all across the country.

I want you to know first of all how greatly Americans admire the heroism of China during these difficult war years. Were it not for the contribution of Chinese soldiers, engineers, universities, and faithful citizens, the task of the United Nations would be very much greater. We are indebted to you, and the United States looks forward to ever closer cooperation with China as she becomes one of the great world powers.

1. THE WAR

Our nations have always been friends, today we are partners in a great war. Neither of us can win alone. Victory looks possible but it is still several years away, and it is not yet clear whether we are willing to pay the price in loyalty and sacrifice. Japan is fundamentally weak, but her conquests have made her geographically strong. She is now both a great maritime power and a continental power as well.

America will do its best to recapture the Pacific islands and destroy the Japanese navy, but the actual invasion and the preliminary bombing will have to come from China. It required 3,000 boats for the Allies to land in Sicily, and Japan will be harder to capture. We may have to put 500,000 men ashore within a few weeks. This can only be done from Shanghai and Tsingtao and Tientsin. China's task is thus to drive out the Japanese army from all of the provinces south of the Great Wall. If you want to know how long the war will last, I would suggest that victory may come within a year after the Chinese armies have recaptured all of the coast line. A large part of our common success thus lies in your hands.

This is a major job, and will require the rehabilitation of the Chinese army. I need not remind you how big a task this will be. Most soldiers today are miserably fed and clothed. They could not possibly use modern equipment even if we could bring it into China, Nor could the rival factions be trusted with such implements afterwards. Instead of illiterate coolies we need trained and intelligent armed forces. Look what a splendid job the rebuilt Chinese army is doing in Burma. It might be better to have fewer and better soldiers, all of them under the central government. And it certainly would be better to have honest generals genuinely true to the central government.

What a wonderful demonstration of loyalty and patriotism it would be if every citizen did his part: rich and poor, students and farmers alike. Even if a quarter of China's college graduates should lose their lives, the contribution to democracy and national unity would be worth while. There is no point in saving the intelligentsia

- 2 -

for reconstruction if we lose the war.

I appreciate how much China has suffered since 1931, and that the army has won many victories, but only the last battle counts. If China becomes war weary before Japan, we lose. And if the war ends today, we have been defeated even though the resistance has been valiant. We must honestly recognize that the Japanese soldiers are better equipped and led as well as more loyal and intelligent, than the Chinese. Although China has fought valiantly, she cannot yet defend herself, let alone take the initiative.

Of course China wants to win, but I have found very few people who are sufficiently concerned to do much about it. Almost no one has spoken to me of China's program for victory. Individuals have experienced great losses, but their reaction is the same as during the struggles of the war lords - this is a personal inconvenience and they hope it will soon end, but they are doing little about it themselves.

China must do its part to win its own war. Just because the United States is now an ally and the Fourteenth Air Force is conducting large operations, this is no time to stop and assume that the end is sure. On the contrary this is the moment to take advantage of such aid. In the years to come it will create an unfortunate psychology if China should have to look back and see that she was not able to unite and work effectively in her hour of peril.

World wide total war finds China seriously unprepared in organization. There may be historic reasons for this, but the results are tragic. We see now what a catastrophe the years of civil war and the failure to develop national consciousness have been. And in the decades ahead we will see the gravity of these present years.

China cannot win by herself. Fortunately we are a part of the United Nations, but China's pride and lack of organization seems to some foreign observers to make her unwilling to accept help and cooperate effectively. The American Army is glad to assist, but in some areas it finds greater problems in dealing with local Chinese officials than with the Japanese. Many of the tasks now undertaken by American soldiers who have come half way round the world to risk their lives could be done by Chinese, if they were willing. The War can be shortened by many months and thousands of lives saved if China will genuinely welcome the participation of the United Nations.

There is too much truth in Japan's assertion that China is a geographical expression rather than a unified nation. If we are to achieve lasting victory, we must first develop national spirit and coherence.

This war is a world wide contest between rival ideas, between a belief in humanity and in dictatorship. We of the democratic nations have put our faith in mankind; we believe that the citizen is more important than the state. The fascist and totalitarian nations believe that the state is more important than the people. The end of the fighting may be near when the armies of China and the United States march down the streets of Tokyo, but the larger aspects of the war will not truly end until the Japanese people come to believe that our way of life is better than theirs. Only then can there be sure peace. This is a long task, and we must demonstrate that our ideals and loyalty are worth while. Only as the United Nations remain united can we achieve this goal.

May I add a few specific suggestions concerning the war. Free China has some excellent blast furnaces and steel mills which are now partly idle. These could make aerial bomb casings and save freight "over the hump"; they could also make cast rails for temporary use on some of the projected railways for which the roadbed is completed, such as the line from Kunming to Burma. A thorough program of truck rehabilitation could make one good car from two or three old ones and greatly aid the serious transportation problem. Universal military service based on ability, eliminating the illiterates, would do a great deal for morale. If the sons of the rich had to serve as privates, their parents would certainly do something about the present treatment of the soldiers. Even though China benefits by certain imports from occupied territory, we should stop sending rice and military commodities to the Japanese. A more realistic news and censorship policy would likewise strengthen public opinion. Inflation is seriously imperiling the war effort and must be stopped, perhaps renewed public confidence in the government is a key.

There have never been so many Americans in China as today, and when they return home they will influence our foreign policy toward this part of Asia. Unfortunately our educational system did not prepare them to understand China or the rest of the world. Some of them appreciate your country, but many others see only dirt and disorder. You can help China by helping them to see the best of your life.

2. R E C O N S T R U C T I O N

China's problems after the war will somewhat resemble those of the Soviet Union during the Five Year Plans, but the differences in background and resources are so marked that it would be unwise to attempt any direct copy of the Soviet program. China must plan, but there are many kinds of planning. Industrial progress is possible under the private capitalism and free initiative of a democracy, witness the strength of the United States, as well as under state socialism. A wise government will leave ample room for competition. China's problem will be to make sure that all sections of the country receive balanced development, and that the essential needs of national security are met. Local regional self sufficiency is impractical and unwise.

The first need is transportation, and this primarily means railways. There will be an immediate demand for hundreds of locomotives and thousands of cars and great amounts of equipment. All of this must come from abroad. Every existing railway will have to be rehabilitated, and within ten years thousands of kilometers of new lines must be built. I regard this as the prime material need in reconstruction. Automobiles and roads are of secondary importance. Some improvements may be made in water transport, but the bulk of commerce will move by rail.

The second need is heavy industry, so that China may make her own rails and chemicals and machines. Heavy industry depends on mining, and mining depends on geology. The National Geological Survey has long been China's outstanding scientific bureau, but it needs to be greatly enlarged. Before there can be any wise planning for industry or for transportation, there must be as complete an inventory of natural resources as possible. A thousand geologists would not be too many, and in many cases international specialists must be brought in.

China is very rich in coal but rather poor in iron, and unfortunately these two are not usually close together nor always near markets. Within the first decade after the war I expect to see three or four spectacular centers of heavy industry, with at least 500-ton blast furnaces in each. China will eventually be the leading industrial area in this part of Asia, although there is little likelihood that she will reach the industrial development of western Europe or eastern North America.

Over-all planning requires the cooperation of many kinds of specialists, but the proper evaluation and interrelation of minerals, land use, communications, settlement and markets is the task of the geographer. Every Soviet planning commission has numerous geographers. It is unfortunate that geography is so undeveloped in China.

China's third problem is agriculture. This is even more important, though perhaps less urgent, than transportation or heavy industry for it directly affects the livelihood of three fourths of the people. This will always remain an agricultural country, and if the standard of living and the national wealth are to be increased, the

- 4 -

condition of the farmer must be greatly improved. Better seeds and better farm management are among the essentials. Very little new land can be cultivated economically. Despite widespread misinformation, both the northwest and the northeast are already full of people in terms of their agricultural capacity. Nowhere in China is there good idle land for more than a few thousand settlers. The agricultural problem must be solved where people already live. Rural reconstruction is the key to a sound China.

Behind this question of agriculture is the greatest of all China's problems: overpopulation. It will do no good to increase agricultural production or improve health if the population continues to rise. Industry will absorb a few million workers, but the bulk will remain farmers.

There are many other problems but I will only mention a fourth, namely export products. Railway equipment and steel mills cost millions of dollars, so too do electric light plants and chemical works. Some of these things can be produced in China within a few years, but even the most urgent post war imports will require hundreds of millions of dollars worth of foreign goods. These will all have to be paid for sooner or later, and will strain China's exchange credit to the limit. If the railways and factories are operated efficiently they will easily pay for themselves, but this may require foreign supervision while the loans are outstanding. China must be prepared to accept foreign partnership in management if she wishes foreign capital.

Once the war is over, many people will again wish to buy fountain pens and automobiles and luxury items. But these consumers goods will also require foreign exchange, and the government may wisely decide to conserve all available credit for producers goods. China will have to tax herself heavily and tighten her belt for another decade or more. Peace will not bring immediate comfort.

The export trade is thus very important. China once had a large market for silk and tea, but these were lost to competitors who produced a more standardized product. The trade in soy beans is also about finished. Tin, tungsten, and antimony are dependable exports but their total value is small. Tung and other vegetable oils, bristles, agricultural products such as eggs, and handicrafts are important, but many others must be found.

Reconstruction is not merely a matter of planning commissions and managed economy. It is worth while only as it starts in the hearts and minds of loyal intelligent citizens, who must be willing to work for it. Such citizens are a nation's greatest resource and bulwork against danger. It is clear that China needs a much greater measure of social organization and national consciousness. This is something which all of her foreign friends earnestly wish. This loyalty cannot be secured by formalism and decree, it must come spontaneously from within, it is not put on like a coat. Patriotism by propaganda never works. Citizens are loyal in proportion as they are free to criticize and to participate in a government which they are proud to call their own.

May I add that these problems of reconstruction are perhaps bigger than some of you realize. During the past decades the rest of the world has made great progress, but despite developments in China, this country is in some ways farther behind than she was earlier. If you are willing to study our mistakes, you may stand on our shoulders and avoid some of them. In any event the rest of us cannot prosper until you have caught up.

Twice in the twentieth century we have learned that there are no wars but world wars, and no world wars but total wars. We must also learn that there is no peace but world peace, and no world peace but total peace. Our planet is now so compact that it cannot live half peaceful and half at war, nor half sick and half well, nor half rich and half poor. We are all in the same boat.

- 5 -

3. FOREIGN RELATIONS

China's location, man power, and coal make it possible for her some day to be one of the Class A powers. She lacks adequate supplies of many minerals, and at present is deficient in technical skill and leadership, but these latter may be changed with time. Prosperous trade and peace in the Pacific community depend on a strong China.

China must decide whether she prefers self-sufficient nationalism or cooperative internationalism. Neither is exclusive of the other, but the decision is fundamental. Before the Second World War, Germany tried to become self-sufficient, but her failure to achieve autarchy was demonstrated when Hitler said that "Germany must export or perish", which meant equally that she had to import. The Soviet Union, which is far richer than China, almost succeeded in becoming economically self-contained but despite her great achievements in the war it is clear that she too has to depend on foreign supplies.

No nation can be strong enough to protect its territory against a combination of enemies, nor can anyone be wise enough to prepare adequately for an unpredictable war yet to come. You cannot protect China by making it a fortress surrounded by another Great Wall, or by regional self sufficiency like the watertight compartments of a ship. Security can come only through collective action on the international side plus loyal intelligent citizens and sound economy on the internal side.

Does internal loyalty and strength need to mean anti-foreignism? How much cooperation will China still welcome in education and business, and in international alliances? China's pre-war foreign contacts were unfortunate in some particulars, though we must recognize that some of the blame falls on both sides. Future loans or business investments need not imply political infringement. China should remember that many of the railways in America were built with European capital, and in part managed from abroad for several decades.

The world is now so small and interdependent that we are truly "under heaven one family". Every culture needs to share its best with every other. We should exchange ambassadors of good will in education, religion, commerce, and agriculture as well as in the diplomatic field. Intelligent good will is one of the surest roads to peace.

You may say that I wish China to have an international policy in order that America may enjoy a large trade. That is true, but I assume that a balanced trade benefits both parties equally. The United States is a high-cost producer and only nations with a high standard of living can afford to buy our exports. It is thus to our enlightened self interest to see China's wealth increase as fast as possible. I also hope that China will continue to welcome western scholars and missionaries, but I equally wish that you would send cultural interpretors to us.

I emphasize all this because along with the great good will for America at the moment, I recognize several fascist tendencies and an apparent unwillingness to understand the West. Only you can decide whether European civilization has values which will prove useful to China, but if China does desire to copy anything from us I am very anxious that you understand the whole of our life as a unit before you choose any part. China must not repeat Japan's great mistake. Japan copied Western science and technology, but completely failed to appreciate Western democracy and the humanities and our spiritual life.

I greatly respect China's ancient virtues, but I believe that they can be enriched by a study of the rest of the world. If Western classics are found to be similar, it will enlarge China's faith in her own past. In any case, it will be unsafe to avoid critical comparison. American life has deep spiritual values as well as material qualities, you cannot borrow one and ignore the other.

This relationship with the west should not be a matter of "face", yet I find that many people in China today have a psychological complex either one way or the other. Those who are pinched by inflation and who are distressed by China's weakness have a feeling of inferiority. Others who are impressed with China's emergence as one of the Big Four of the United Nations have a superiority complex. Neither attitude is justified; perhaps these are merely the inevitable difficulties when an old culture long dominant in its own sphere discovers another world of ideas and values.

I think of many specific problems. Some concern the United States, the Soviet Union or the British Commonwealth; others deal with a defeated Japan. For example, how do you propose to administer Formosa, how shall we punish Japan and yet make it possible for her to eventually regain face as a neighbor? What is the future of colonial Asia, including China's outer territories? I hesitate to introduce imperialism, but all of the great powers have shown expansionist tendencies and China is no exception. China already has several million advance agents in Southeastern Asia and her program of emigration and trade will sooner or later result in political problems. The Chinese in Thailand are even less popular than foreigners have sometimes been in China! What is China's idea about the freedom of the air and international bases?

Or take the case of Hongkong versus Canton. Just as soon as Canton develops sufficient trade, commercial facilities, and an adequate harbor, ocean-going ships will prefer to come there. Political considerations are secondary. It is not honest for us to use past or existing treaty situations as a cover for domestic conditions. Foreign imperialism must take its blame, but it is not responsible for all of China's internal difficulties.

Neither China nor any other nation alone can solve these international problems. The only safe procedure is through consultation. What is needed now is a genuine willingness to cooperate on the part of the Chinese people as a whole. I believe that I can assure you of America's continued friendship. Our countries each have a great deal of good will for the other, but it must become more intelligent on both sides.

4. GOVERNMENT

When the Nationalist Government came into power in 1928, it was a liberal movement which commanded the enthusiastic support of the intelligentsia. Today it has swung to the extremely conservative side, perhaps in self defense, and has lost the support of many of the people who once worked for it. The Kuomintang provided a totalitarian rule from the start, but whereas it once was liberal it has become increasingly fascist. Many people are thus doubtful whether one-party rule will ever be willingly relinquished. The problem is not merely that China is more and more bureaucratic, that may happen under a democratic system. The problem lies in not building from the bottom up; the citizen is told, not asked.

The two great issues are assumed to be fascism and communism, but there is inadequate consideration of the middle ground of democracy. China is one of the most socially democratic of all lands. Full political democracy may be impractical for a generation but there is not now enough attention to the individual's place in government. Why is it that in discussing the new constitution, the newspapers in one province are reported to be forbidden to use the word democracy?

Too much power is in the hands of a few people, several of whom are fundamentally weak and who misuse power to protect themselves. China has many able men, but not enough of them are competent statesmen. This is one of her major difficulties. The true leader must secure his position through respect and hold it by ability, not by the misuse of force.

The present program of the Kuomintang appears to an outsider to be too much surrounded by military regimentation and nazi ideas. While most people in foreign countries are uninformed about this problem, I must tell you frankly that many friends of China are seriously concerned about the increasingly dictatorial character of the government. There must be a constitutional corrective which will truly be above party.

Perhaps a part of this situation is America's fault. When Sun Yat-sen started the Nationalist movement, he first turned to the United States government for aid, but they replied that we could not assist revolutions in countries with whom we were on friendly diplomatic terms. So Dr. Sun was forced to turn to the Russians, with the resulting problem of communism. Again when China needed advice in the early part of the war with Japan, she was obliged to seek help from Germany, from which came the heritage of nazi ideology.

China must not have another civil war, and it is a serious mistake for people to assume that is is inevitable. Such a war would be tragic for China's livelihood, it might set back reconstruction for a decade, it would imperil China's reservoir of friendship abroad, and might even initiate another world war. It can almost certainly be avoided if we wish. One alternative is to make the government of the Kuomintang so powerful that it can easily crush the Communists and remaining war lords. This is what the United States Army is unconsciously doing in the war with Japan. But power is dangerous if uncontrolled. Another alternative is to make the central government so able and attractive that it will win the support of the majority of the people. Genuine widespread loyalty can be the only basis for a permanent government. The first question is not whether the Communists will disband their army and join in constitutional government if invited, the first problem is to deflate their ideas by raising a banner to which the bulk of the citizens will choose to rally.

This means freedom of speech and of the press, freedom from gestapo censorship, open criticism of the government both constructive and destructive, fewer restraints on personal liberty, and as much representative government as the educational standards permit. This will require courage; courage to believe that people of right should rule themselves and that they can learn to do so, courage to insist that the citizen is more important than the state, a belief that humanity is above all.

5. EDUCATION

A university is one of the corner stones of good government and a major safeguard of liberty. Its research supports agriculture and industry, and its contribution to character helps to create good citizens. But a university must be free. Academic freedom is no mere pleasant luxury for the secluded scholar, it is essential for all progress.

The great universities of Germany ceased to be of service when their teachers were told what they could or could not teach. Party doctrines have no place in objective scholarship except as comparative examples. A true university exists for the common good of all mankind, certainly not for propaganda. Regimentation and standardization kill initiative. It is better to have a dozen inferior teachers or colleges and leave them free in the hope that one will develop creative ideas than to try to lift them all to some minimum standard by decree.

There is too much tendency in Chinese education to insist on the externals of orderliness, such as military discipline, neat dormitories and political ceremonies, rather than intellectual integrity, devotion to the truth, and social consciousness. Students must learn to think for themselves rather than merely conform to a pattern. One of the problems of China's earlier literary education was that it led to talk rather than to action. New situations have now arisen which call for resourcefulness.

- 8 -

Education is properly the concern of local, provincial and national government, but there must also be opportunity for private schools at all levels. No central government anywhere is wise enough to satisfy all the requirements of a varied society. There must be the freedom and experimentation which only private schools can provide. China has many millionaires, and private philanthropy should be encouraged to support education.

Here is a very genuine problem in war time China. Inflation has brought tragic consequences to many teachers with results for which the country will pay dearly for a generation. Without financial aid from the Ministry of Education many schools would have closed. Incidentally, some of the universities still open should close as they have ceased to make any contribution. There are already more national universities than the central government can support, yet pressure is brought to add more. What is even more serious, the number of strong private universities is decreasing.

Post war plans should look forward to the return of many universities to provincial or private control. The function of a Ministry of Education in any country, like that of a private Board of Trustees, should be to supervise the finances and physical plant but leave matters of educational policy to scholars. If it does have an academic mission it should be to set ideals but not force conformity. Uniformity and regimentation are dangerous; liberal education needs initiative in research and teaching, experimentation, and local flexibility. China unfortunately has many sub-standard universities, but society seldom needs to be told which institutions are doing acceptable work.

It is perhaps just as well that students are no longer engaged in political agitation, but I wish that they showed an equally active concern over something - whether their own studies or China's social problems or the war. Nowhere have I found more than a very minor interest in communism.

Although the number of college students has considerably increased during the war period, the number of competent teachers has decreased and the supply of new instructors has almost stopped. This shortage of scholars is one of the most critical educational problems. Since it will not be possible to offer satisfactory graduate work leading to the doctorate within China for several years, additional teachers must be trained abroad. Thousands are needed at once. Part of the deficiency may be met by bringing more foreigners to China for graduate instruction, but such advanced work would require books and equipment not now available.

This raises the whole problem of foreign study. No country is content with imported education, yet for the present there is little alternative for China. And in a way this cultural interchange is fortunate for Chinese students abroad have contributed greatly to their country's diplomatic good will. China's problem of catching up with the West is made much simpler by the returned student, even though some may be partial failures. It would be equally valuable if hundreds of American college students might spend some time in China, say their Junior year in Peiping. Such student interchange should be helped in every way possible, but it must be free from indoctrination courses or supervision of ideas. And it must not be restricted to those approved by any board of censorship on either side.

The universities of Free China deserve great credit for their service under very great handicaps. At the same time the quality of their work has deteriorated greatly, perhaps to 50 per cent of its pre-war value. This is due to such factors as inadequate libraries and laboratory equipment, the decline of faculty and student morale and health on account of inflation, the curtailment of valuable extra-curricular activities, and the prescription by Chungking of too many required courses.

In view of this war time deterioration of the bachelor's degree, almost all students going abroad after the war should repeat their Senior and possibly Junior year, preferably in a small college in a small town. Within a decade it should again be unnecessary for more than a handfull of Chinese undergraduates to study abroad, but the door must not be closed to them too soon. Foreign study will use up precious foreign exchange, but this is a fundamental investment in the future of China. Nothing else will pay as large dividends.

China's educational needs are manifold. The country urgently requires more engineers and chemists and all sorts of technicians. But she also needs economists and psychologists and government officials. If a big engineering job presents difficulties it is possible to hire a foreign specialist, but if the government is confronted with major political problems China must produce her own statesmen. I am convinced that the greatest needs are not skills but character, loyalty and courage. The engineers are already doing a magnificent job under difficulty. We shall need many more but it is clear that the technical jobs can be done. Whether China can equally solve her political and social problems is more uncertain and more fundamental.

The old cultural pattern of China has been broken up by her discovery of the outside world, and the new loyalty and way of life have not yet appeared. There needs to be an appreciation of the unity of all truth and a new organization of knowledge in order to provide a suitable basis for behavior as world citizens. Present-day students are seriously lacking in such a philosophy.

It will not be enough merely to preserve China's classical virtues and add American science. There must be a reevaluation of all her way of life in terms of her new world relations. And social changes require more wisdom and patience than material changes. In the larger view, the political scientist and social worker has a more fundamental problem than the physicist or technician.

This means that Colleges of Arts are more important than Colleges of Engineering. Perhaps it would be better to say that engineers need character and humanitarian understanding quite as much as engineering ability. In sending students abroad, quite as many should study the liberal arts as the applied sciences.

China has a unique advantage in that American and European friends have been willing to found and support colleges in this country. The contribution of these Christian universities to international understanding and spiritual values should be welcomed and encouraged. And to my American friends I wish to say that if these universities are to continue, their standards must be materially raised. We should send the very finest teachers in all of the United States, and make it possible for our Chinese associates to travel abroad more freely. These schools should combine the best of the west with the best of China. No one should be able to say that they were out of tune with China. Other universities may need to train large numbers of students without emphasis upon superior quality, but the Christian universities must maintain the highest standards, both in intellectual integrity and social character.

Education is made up of two parts. One we may call scholarship, the other is less easily defined or taught for it deals with personality and the development of character. Most Chinese universities are too little concerned with the life of their students outside the class room. Great universities require great teachers, and I may again repeat that I consider China's outstanding needs to be character, loyalty, and courage.

This is a total war, and education must make its specialized contribution to victory. Today is not the time for universities to continue as usual, so that what I have written above refers to normal situations. Chinese college men are now almost the only male students in any major country who are still able to study as they please.

- 10 -

How will they feel when confronted with men of their generation from other lands? American students have had to leave their college life and come to China to defend this country, so that this is no time for Chinese students to go abroad.

If China is to earn her own victory, she must train thousands of army specialists - aviators, radio operators, artillery officers, interpretors, engineers, administrators. Chinese universities should at once go on a war basis. Perhaps this country may even wish to ask the American army to take over a university campus, bring in western teachers and equipment, and train college men for army service as a demonstration of what we are doing in the United States.

-:-:-:-:-:-:-

Written during a beautiful week on Omei Shan in 1944.

1944年
葛德石致中国人民书（中文版）

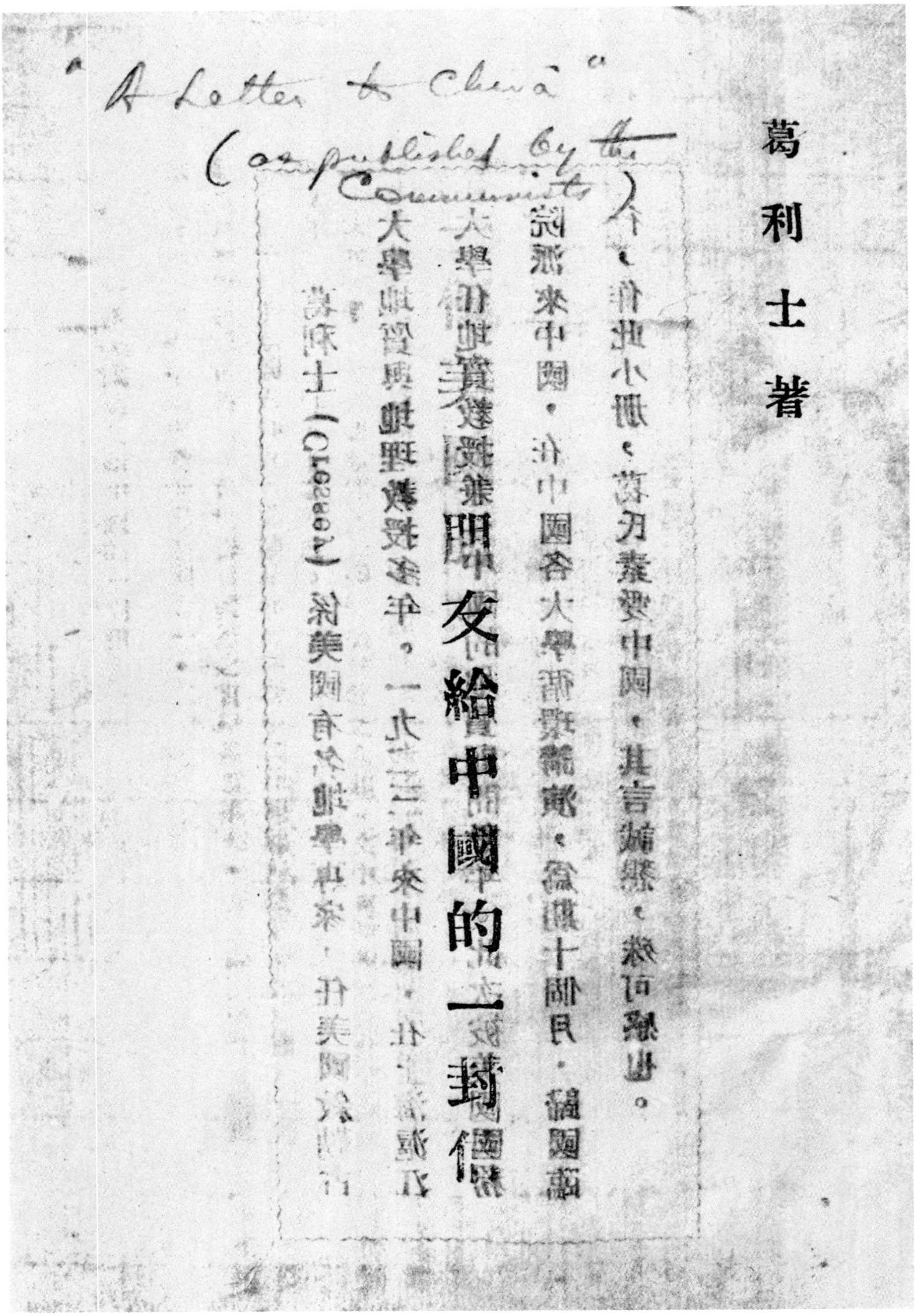

"A Letter to China"
(as published by the Communists)

葛利士著

葛利士（Cressey）係美國有名地學專家，任美國敘勒古大學地質與地理教授多年。一九二三年來中國，在上海滬江大學任地質教授兼任中國的地質顧問數年。此次被美國國務院派來中國，在中國各大學循環講演，爲期十個月，歸國臨行，作此小册，葛氏素愛中國，其言誠懇，殊可感也。

一個美國朋友給中國的一封信

今日爲中國革命後最重要之時期，但機會愈大，其嚴重性亦愈多，若吾人循正當之路前進，則將來必關光明，而中國亦將成爲世界領袖國家之一。如吾人於此種之努力失敗，則將影響整個世界，我既與奮，亦感失望。吾人的確需要智慧與勇氣與透視的觀察。我係以一個中國之忠實朋友的態度而寫此文。我要讀者了解我所說者爲何，而非欲讀者知道我是誰人，故我不具名此信，我熟知中國甚久，（居住中國若干年）最近數月內我曾旅行九省。我不欲述所有一切優點，也不批評缺點，我將分析問題，與提供解決問題之建議。我雖然爲一美國人而寫出此文，我亦可認爲係中國之一分子，現今世界是如此其小而互相依賴。此間所發生之一切事件，均將影響其餘之人類。文中有些爲我自己之意見，然大部份均爲得自與各處千百人士之談話。

首先我要請讀者知道，美國是如何稱讚中國在此艱苦戰爭中之忍勇，中國之士兵，機師，大學生與誠實公民，對於聯合國家之貢獻甚爲偉大。吾人感激中國，美國且願與中國嚴密合作，以使中國成爲世界強國之一。

一個美國朋友給中國的一封信

一，戰　爭

中美兩國久為朋友，今日復係一偉大戰爭中之夥伴，吾人均不能單獨獲勝，勝利雖已屬可能，但尚須經歷數年，目前我們尚不明白我們是否願意以忠心與犧牲作為勝利的代價。日本本質雖屬脆弱，但其初勝利則已使之取得地理的優勢，日本今日已兼為海洋與大陸的強國。

美國將竭盡所能以重佔太平洋各島，與催毀日本的海軍，惟實際侵入日本與初步的轟炸，均須從中國發動。盟軍登陸西西里島使用三千艘船隻，佔領日本自遠較艱難。此項登陸行動，只能從上海青島及天津等地為之，華軍之任務即在將日軍從長城以南之各省逐出。如讀者欲知戰爭將於何時結束，我可以提供一個答覆，勝利將在華軍收復所有海岸線後一年後得。吾人大部份的成功因素，乃在中國人的手中。

重建中國軍隊，確為一主要工作，亦且為一巨大的任務，大多數的中國士兵，均在泥陸之中，他們不能使用現代的裝備，即使吾人能將現代裝備運至中國，此種軍隊亦復不能倚托。吾人需要有訓練與有智識之軍隊來代替不識字之苦力。新建之中國軍隊正作戰於緬甸，其表現至為優良。由此可知兵貴精而不貴多。若中國有精兵良將又能指揮統一，則勝利可計日而待也。

每一公民如窮人與富翁，學生與農民，均各盡其本分，則忠心與愛國之表現必將放一異彩，即使只有四分之一。中國大學畢業生爲民主與統一而犧牲其生命亦屬值得之事，蓋如吾人之戰爭失敗，則重建中國所需之智識份子亦無法尚全也。

我深知中國在一九三一年後即遭受苦難。中國軍隊已獲得若干勝利，惟只有最後一戰始能結算總債。若中國感到戰爭之疲憊較日本爲早，則吾人即屬失敗矣。吾人必須誠實的承認，日軍裝備較華軍爲優，並較華軍富於忠心與智慧。華軍雖作戰英勇，但不能保衛自身，幷缺乏單獨的創造力。

自然，中國是在要求勝利，但却很少有中國人是在充分的做獲得勝利的工作，甚至無人曾經告訴我中國對於獲得勝利的計劃。

中國人民在戰爭中遭受鉅大的損失，但彼等的反應仍與軍閥鬥爭時一樣——僅爲一種人事之紛爭。人民希望戰爭很快結束，但彼等對此却甚少努力。

當美國現正爲中國的盟友，而十四航空隊又正在進行其偉大之表演時，中國必須竭力作戰以求勝利，現在絕非停止行動而相信戰爭快將結束的時期。反之，此時正爲利用美國援助加緊作戰的最好時機。假若中國在數年後返觀現在而覺得她不能在她危急存亡之秋就

一個美國朋友給中國的一封信　　四

而有效的工作，則將使世界對她發生一種不幸的心理。

全球廣大全面的戰爭，已考驗出中國在組織上毫無準備，此或許有其歷史之原因，而其結果則爲一悲劇，現在吾人可以看出連年內戰與國家意識之未能發展是如何的一種危機。在此後十年中，吾人將可以看出最近幾年的嚴重後果。

中國不能藉其一己之力獲勝。幸好吾人均爲聯合國家的一分子。但是中國之傲慢與缺之組織，此種情勢，使有些外國觀察者看來，彷彿表示中國不願接受援助與真實合作。美國士兵極高興幫助中國，但在有些地方發生許多問題，使美軍應付中國地方官吏，還較應付日本軍隊爲困難。跋涉半個地球，並冒生命危險的美軍，現已與華軍同樣的從事此一偉大工作。如中國願意，並真誠歡迎聯合國之參加，則此戰爭將縮短若干月之時間，與節約若干人之生命。

日本斥中國爲一地理名詞，而非一統一國家，其言實非常真實。如吾人欲求得最後之勝利，必須首先發揚民族精神與增加國家之團結。

此次戰爭爲世界兩相反觀念之全面抗爭。乃信仰人道與信仰獨裁者之戰爭。吾人爲民主國家，忠實於全體人類。吾人相信人民重於國家，法西斯與極權國家則相信國家高於人民。菲軍與美軍進於東京市街時，戰爭可云結束，但在日本人民相信吾人之生活方式（民主）較彼等爲優以前，戰爭實不能眞正完結。必須在上述之條件下始能有眞正之和平。此乃一長期之工作，吾人必須使吾人之忠心與信念均能發揮其價值。聯合國僅能在聯合之努力中，始能獲得此一目的。

關於戰爭，我再提供少數特別之建議，自由中國有許多煉鐵爐與鋼鐵廠，現均閒散未用，此等設備如能製造炸彈外殼，則可減少美國空運越過「駝峯」之重負。此等設備亦能製造輕便鐵軌，以暫時用於業已設計之鐵道，此等鐵道之路基現已完成，如昆明至緬甸之路綫，一重建之貨車運輸計劃，能從兩三輛舊車造成一輛好車，此必大有助於解決嚴重之運輸問題，一切軍事工作均需要才幹，掃除文盲，可以提高軍隊素質。假如富家子弟都能從軍，則渠等之父母必將盡力於士兵待遇之改善。

從淪陷區輸入某些物資對於中國雖屬有利，但吾人應禁止把米糧與軍用物品送給日本。一個較翔實的新聞報導與進步的檢查制度，將更加強輿論的力量。通貨膨脹使戰鬥力大受損害，必須迅予停止。重建政府之信用，或爲挽救通貨膨脹的關鍵。

美人之在中國者從無今日之多，彼輩返國時，將影響美國之遠東外交政策。不幸美國之教育制度，未曾預先準備，使此等美人能了解中國或其他各地。彼等有部份甚爲讚賞中國，但大多數均只見及汚濁與無秩序。讀者若能幫助美人，使之能看到中國人生活之最好的一面，則君等即已幫助中國矣。

二，戰後建設

中國之戰後問題，或將類似蘇聯之五年計劃。惟因歷史背景與資源之顯著不同，直接抄襲蘇聯之政策，乃極不聰明之事。中國必須要計劃，但計劃有許多種類。工業的進步，可以在私人資本主義與民主政治下之自由創造而實現。吾人可以美國之富強為例證。美國人亦與國家社會主義者有同樣之成就，聰明之政府必須多留競爭的餘地。中國之問題是在使國家各部分均得平衡發展，并使國家安全的目的得以達到。區域之自給自足既辦不到，亦不聰明。

第一需要為運輸，初步之方法為鐵路。中國戰後將立即需要成百之機關車與成千之列車，以及大量之設備。凡此均須來自外國。每條已成的鐵路必須恢復，並尚須在十年之內建築若干公里之新幹綫。此乃為戰後建設最基本之物質需要。其次要者為公路與汽車。水運或可獲得若干之進步，但主要之商業仍須倚賴鐵路運輸。

第三需要為重工業。由此中國可以自己建造鐵路、化學工廠與機器。至工業所賴鑛業，鑛業則有賴於地質學。國家地質調查局久為中國卓著之科學機關，但尚須大加充實。中

關於建立工業與運輸之良好計劃以前，必須儘可能的完成國家資源之總調查，一千個地質學家將不算多，并須由各種方式，邀請國際專家。中國煤藏豐富缺之鐵產，此二者之產區既不密集，又不靠近市場。戰後最初十年中，我希望能看到三個或四個之特殊之重工業中心區，至少每一區均有日產五百噸之煉鐵爐，中國雖不能達到歐洲或東部北美工業發展之程度，而終將成為東亞之工業領導區。

在一切計劃之上，需要各種專家之合作，推適量之估計，礦脈間相互之關係，土地之用法，與交通之路理及市場之位置等，皆屬地理學家之任務。每一蘇維埃計劃委員會，均有無數之地理學家，不幸地理學在中國却並不如此發達。

中國第三問題為農業，此較諸運輸或重工業或屬不甚緊急，然却較為重要。因為農業直接關係四分之三以上人民之生計，中國仍將永為農業國家。如生活水準與國民財富增高，則農民之情況亦必可獲巨大之改進。優良之種子與較好之耕種方法，厥為此問題中之最主要者。中國可耕地面積甚廣，乃係誤傳。絕少有新的土地，可供較經濟的耕種，在西北與東北，沃土亦已住滿居民。以此等之農業技術言之，中國實已無足供容納數千人以上居住之肥沃而未使用之土地。中國之農業問題，必須在人民已經居住之地方謀求解決。復興農村乃為健康中國之鎖鑰。農業問題有後存在中國最大之困難問題為人口過剩。如人口繼繼續增長，將無法增加農業生產與改善人民健康。工業只能容納幾百萬工人，而大多數人民仍須留住農村。

此外尚有若干問題，我只再提出一、第四問題，即出口貨之生產。鐵路器材與鋼鐵工廠，需要千百萬之美元，電氣事業與化學工廠亦需耗費鉅量之金錢。有些物品在幾年內中國能夠自己生產。但是戰後最切需的進口貨價值當亦不下數萬萬美元。此等借款或現交或緩付，將使中國之外匯迅速消耗至其限度。設若鐵路與工廠之管理甚有效率，則彼等之債款或容易自己負擔。外債數目如極鉅大，外國或將要求關會與監督。中國需要外資，必須於管理方面準備接受外國合夥公司之制度。

戰爭結束後許多人民將欲重購自來水筆、汽車及奢侈品，此等消費品亦將消耗外匯，政府應聰明的決定，保存對生產物資之有效信用。在戰後之十年或更長之時期中，中國須對其自身徵收重稅，加強節約，和平并不能即時帶來舒服。

出口貿易極其重要，中國曾經一度保持絲茶之廣大市場，惟已在標準較高之生產競爭中喪失其地位，大豆貿易亦復將完結，錫鎢銻鉍均爲可靠之出口貨物，但其總值甚屬微小，桐油及其他之植物油豬鬃鷄蛋及手工藝品等均極重要。但其他更可爲之生產事業亦須確立起來。

戰後之重建，不僅爲計劃委員會之要務，經濟之管理，其價值須發自忠心與智慧之公民心理中，吾等須充分願意爲此工作而努力，此輩公民，爲國家最大之資源，亦爲對抗危機之最大力量。中國需要大量之社會組織與國民自覺，實至爲顯然，此亦爲所有外國友人所渴望之事。此種忠心不能爲形式主義與命令所保持，必須由內心自發，非若外衣之可隨便加上，由宣傳而來之愛國心，從不發生作用。公民之忠心，乃與自由批評與參加政治之程度成正比例。蓋如是公民始能感覺自家——國家乃自己之國家。

戰後重建問題，或較一般人所想像者爲鉅大，過去十年中，其他各地均有長足之進步。中國不特沒有進步，有些方面或反較從前大爲落後。設若中國願意研究吾人的錯誤，則中國可以借吾人前車之鑑而避免後車之覆。假若中國不能迎頭趕上，其餘的世界也不能獨享繁榮。

二十世紀中，吾人業已兩次學知世界一有戰爭，即成爲一世界戰爭，一有世界戰爭，即是全面戰爭。我們也應該學知：無世界和平，即無和平，無全體和平，即無世界和平。吾人之地球，現今極爲密接，不能一半在戰爭中過活，一半又生活於和平之中。也不能一半生在貧病之中，一半又生在富裕之中，我們大家有如同舟共濟，必須相依爲命。

中國以其地力，人力，及其煤鐵，可能經過相當時日，成爲頭等列強之一。中國缺乏足量的鑛源，中國今日尤其缺乏專門技術人材與領袖，惟此將爲時間而改變。太平洋上之和平興盛的貿易，乃倚賴一強大之中國。

三，對外關係

中國必須決定，究採「自給自足主義」或「國際合作主義」。此兩者均非絕對互不相容，但決心仍屬緊要。此次大戰之前，德國曾企圖變成自給自足之國家，但當希特拉宣稱：「德國必需出口貿易，不然即是滅亡」一語時，即已證明其努力已遭受失敗。蘇聯這較中國爲富裕，在經濟上幾乎足以完全自給，但在此次作戰之際雖成就甚多，仍必須仰賴外國之供應。

無任何一國，能有足夠之力量，以對抗聯合之敵人，而保衞其領土，吾人亦不能有充分之才智，可以確切準備一不可預料與尚未到來之戰爭。中國不能建築另外一個長城式之堡壘，環繞四境，保衞國土。中國亦不能若船上不漏水之房間以自給自足。安全之獲得，一方面在國際之有集體的行動，一方面在國內之有忠實的公民及健全的經濟。

忠於國家，富強本國，是否即須含有排外主義？中國在教育上，商業上，與國際同盟中接受合作的程度究有幾何？中國戰前之對外接觸，在有些特殊方面，頗爲不幸。惟吾人必須認識，此種過失雙方均有責任。將來之貸款與商業投資，不僅需要政治默契，中國必須記着美國許多鐵路均由外資建築，並且一部份由外國管理好幾十年。

今日之世界極其微小，彼此互相依賴，吾人雖屬「天下一家」。各種文化均須以其優良之成就貢獻與他人。吾人在教育，宗教，商務以及農業等方面亦須互派訪問代表，若外交方面之大使一樣。智慧之交流，乃一條達到和平之可靠道路。

讀者或將謂：予欲藉中國之國際政策以使美國享受巨量之貿易利益。此言確係真實。但我敢保證，平衡之貿易，其利益在雙方均係相等。美國爲一成本甚高之生產國家，只有生活水準較高之國家，始有力購買美國貨物。中國財富迅速增加，始能增加美國利益，我希望將來中國繼續歡迎西方之學者與教士，我亦同樣盼望中國能派遣文化之傳譯者至美國。

我對此極其重視，中美此刻之友誼甚篤。惟我認定少數有法西斯傾向者與皮指之士，卻不願充分了解美國。只有你們中國人民自己能決定歐洲文明對中國有無價值。但中國人抄襲吾人任何事物時，我熱忱盼望，在選擇時，須要了解吾人生活之整體，中國應勿重錯日本之大錯：日本抄襲西方之科學與專門技術，而未體會西方之民主政治、古代文學與精神生活。

我極為尊敬中國古代之美德，但我亦相信學習其他各國，將益增美好。如於西方經典中察出相同之處，更可加強中國對其過去之信心。無論何事，避免比較之批評，即不妥當。美國人之生活，亦有極深厚之精神價值，如美國人之物質生活一樣，中國人不能僅其一種而捨去他面。

中國與西方之關係，不應僅屬表面之事物，我今日已從中國各方面發現一種心惡的「情意綜」。有些人為通貨膨脹所困，為國勢微弱所苦，遂為「自卑的情意綜」所愚弄。有些人因為中國一躍而為同盟四強之一，不免又具有「自高的情意綜」。這兩種態度都不對；這也許僅是一種長期故步自封的舊文化，一旦發現別人也有理想與價值的世界時所應有的困難。

我思索許多特殊的問題，或係關於美國蘇聯，或者關於不列顛聯邦，或其他關於日本戰敗之問題。譬若中國如何計劃以管理台灣，吾人如何懲治日本，而使之仍能回復其鄰人之面目？亞洲殖民地之將來如何（此包括中國之國外領土），我並非介紹帝國主義，但所有大國均已表示其擴張領土之趨勢，而中國也未例外。中國在東南亞洲已有幾百萬之先鋒隊，中國之移民與貿易計劃，將不久在政治方面得一決策，中國人在泰國較諸有一時期外國人之在中國者更不待人望，不知中國對於空中自由與國際基地之觀念如何？

吾人試以香港對於廣州而論，如廣州之貿易充分發達，有巨大之商店與適宜之港口，則外輪將寧願駛抵廣州，政治之攷慮乃屬次要，吾人利用過去或已存之條約情勢，干涉中國內政，乃極不誠實之行為。外國之帝國主義，固應遭受非難，惟亦並不對所有中國國內之困難負其全責。

中國或其他任何一國，均不能單獨解決國際問題，解決國際問題最安全之程序厥為協議，繼續擴大對中國全體人民之善意合作，極為需要。我相信我能保證美國必將繼續其對中國之友誼。中美兩國彼此均有好感，但雙方必須更行增進其智慧。

四，政府

國民黨政府於一九二八年取得政權時，他是一個為智識階級熱忱支持的自由運動。他在今日已退步至絕端保守之境，此或係由於自衛，與乎失掉大量曾經一度從事自由運動者的支持。國民黨於其獲權之初，即建立一極權的統治，以是，自由主義即漸變為日益增長之法西斯蒂，大多數人民均極懷疑，一黨專政將會自願放棄？中國之問題不是逐漸官僚化，而是應建立一種民主之制度。中國的民主運動不是自下而上，人民是被動的而非自動的。

法西斯與共產主義二者間有最大之爭端，但中立人民所考慮而願採取者，乃爲民主政治。中國社會之民主程度最高，惟完全之政治民主則從來未曾練習。並且今日政府，迄不承認個人之地位，在憲政硏討聲中，某省之報紙竟被禁止使用民主二字，政府態度乃如是也。

極少數人掌握極大之權力，渠輩中數人之本質又庸弱無能，幷借公以營私，中國才智之士甚多，而皆無足夠爲政治家之資格。此乃中國一主要之困難，眞正之領袖保持其地位，必須由於人民之尊敬與信任，其獲得權勢亦應由於其本身之才幹而不應憑藉武力。

國民黨今日之政策所表現於外人眼中者，爲過分的軍事部勒與納粹觀念，此爲大多數來華的外國人所不深悉的實情，我坦白的告訴讀者，中國之許多外國友人，對於中國政府獨裁性之日益增加，表示嚴重之憂慮，中國政府必須根據憲政原則加以改進，而老老實實的不要以一黨一派的利益爲前提。

吾人或可云造成此種情勢之原因，一部份是由於美國之錯誤與過失。當孫逸仙博士開始其國民黨運動時，首先向美國政府要求協助。而美國政府答稱，「吾人不能在邦交友善之國家內援助革命」。以是孫先生卽被迫轉而求助於俄國，遂發生聯俄容共的結果，後來中國在早期中日戰爭時需要顧問，乃又迫向德國尋求協助，於是中國即從德國獲得納粹理論的遺產。

中國不能再發生內戰，目前已使人民認爲內戰乃不可避免之事，確爲嚴重之錯誤。內戰只有爲中國之民生帶來悲劇，只有將戰後重建工作就延十年，且將喪失外國對中國積累多年之友誼，並可能引起另一次世界戰爭。假若吾人願意，內戰當能避免。一個辦法，就是使國民黨政府有強大的權力足以輕易的把共產黨與殘餘軍閥消滅於無形，援華抗日的美軍或者正在不知不覺的做着這種工作。但是政府的權力如無限制，乃確屬危險之事。故另一較妥的辦法，就是使中央政府有能幹，有信用，以期獲得多數人民的擁護與支持。眞誠與普徧的忠心，爲政府長治久安的唯一基礎。中國之先決問題，不是共產黨應解散軍隊而被請加入政府，而是取消彼此令人選擇黨徽的觀念。

中國人民需要言論與出版之自由，需要無特務機關檢查之自由，人民能公開批評政府，不論其意見爲建設性的，或破壞性的，對於人身自由要少加干涉，應提高教育程度，并成立代議政治。此則需要勇氣，尤其需要勇氣相信人民有權統治自己，人民應學習統治自己。更要有勇氣堅信人民重於國家，人性高於一切。

五，教育

大學爲優良政府柱石之一，亦爲自由之重要保障。其研究所得供給農業與工業，其全部之貢獻更有助於良好公民德性之培養。但是大學必須自由，學術自由不特是悟道的學者應有的權利，也是一切進步的原素。德國的著名大學當其教授們被命令何者應教何者不應教的時候，就失掉他們的重要性。政黨的主張在學位之取得上並無位置，僅可用以作爲比較研究的例證，一個眞正的大學，乃爲全人類的共同福利而存在，絕非用作宣傳與佈置。「編制與標準」祇有摧毀人類的創造能力。一般次等之教師與學校，如能有自由講學與研究之機會，則必能發展，等創造之觀念，實較一般嚴守功令與標準化之教師與大學爲佳。

中國教育現正強烈趨向於表面化與形式之整齊，例如着重軍事訓練，內務整理，以及紀念週等，此等事務反較重於智力之充實與保持，以及眞理之信仰，與社會之自覺。學生實應學習爲自己而思想，不僅以服從一種模型爲能事。中國學生必須認識中國從前特重文學教育所發生的問題，這種教育是易於坐而言而難於起而行。今日中國處於新形勢中，她需要應變濟世的人才。

教育自爲地方政府省政府及中央政府所應辦的事，惟亦須由各級私立學校以發展之機會。沒有任何國家的中央政府，能完全滿足多變的社會的一切要求。祇有私立學校方有足夠的自由來作種種實驗。中國有許多百萬富翁與私家慈善機關，均應鼓勵他們來維護教育。

中國戰時之一真正問題，為通貨膨脹，他使多數教師陷入於悲慘之境地。國家為救濟教員，所支出者實較從來為多，多數學校如無教育部財政部之補助即將停閉。但若干大學已無任何貢獻，而應停閉者，却仍然存在，此殊出人意料之外。國立大學之多，實已超出國民政府所能負担之能力，而此種困難，尚在日益增加，中國今日之最嚴重者，無過於優良之私立大學日趨減少。

戰後設計，必須仍令多數大學由省政府或私人管理。其他國家之教育部有若一個私人之信託部，負供給財政與物質設計之責，而將教育政策付諸學者，如果要提出一個大學的任務，則只宜提出一些理想，而不應强迫學生依樣畫葫蘆。整齊劃一與嚴格控制卽是危險。自由教育，需要教學雙方之創造性，實驗，以及因地制宜。中國不幸有若干在標準以下之大學，但是社會用不着別人告訴他，就會知道那個大學在做着他所歡迎的工作。

學生今日似已不再參與政治的騷動，但我願意他們轉移目標注意別的事情——如彼等自身之學問，中國之社會問題以及與抗戰有關之問題等。中國學生對於共產主義與趣之淡，是我在別處所未發現的。

戰時大學生之數目雖顯著增加，而優良之教師則日趨減少，新教師之補充似乎業已斷絕。學者之如此缺乏，乃是一個最迫急的教育問題。因爲中國大學畢業生不能在國內從事獲得博士學位之研究工作，故新聘之教師，必須在外國訓練。此刻立即需要成千之教師。此一部份可藉外國學者來華主持研究機構以培養之，惟此類深造工作，需要圖書與設備，此在目前則屬不可能之事。

於此即又發生一「留學問題」。無任何一國甘以舶來品教育自滿，然在中國目前雖此爲無別的替代辦法，就一方面言，中國派遣學生出洋與外國交換文化乃爲幸事，因爲中國留學生已爲中國獲得許多外交好感。歸國的學生，雖有一部份失敗，必將使中國很快的迎頭趕上西方的文化。如數百美國大學生能在中國居住若干時日，或即在北平讀其低年級之學程，則此必與中國學生留學有相等之價值，中外交換學生應當獲得多方面之協助，惟此必須自由，不指定學科與控制思想，並且不受任何方面檢查制度之拘束。

自由中國之大學在極度困難下工作，實應獲得最大之信譽。惟在此期間內，彼等工作之品質則大爲退化。或可云僅及戰前之一半，此乃由於缺乏圖書館與實驗室之設備，學生因通貨膨脹而智識道德與健康，均日趨衰退，以及減少有價值之選修課程所致。

戰時大學畢業生之成績極其低劣，彼等若戰後留學，應該在美國重讀其三四年級或者即讀一二年級之課程，最好在一個小城而規模不大的大學中，在戰後十年內未畢業的大學生出國留學或不甚需要，但門不能關得太早。留學雖必須使用大宗外匯，然此乃中國最根本之投資，其所得之紅利，亦較任何投資爲大。

中國教育之需要爲多方面的。中國急需大量之工程師與化學家以及其他各種專門人才。她亦需要經濟學家，心理學家與政府官吏。如一巨大之機械工程發生困難，可以求助於外國專家，但若政府發生重要之政治問題，則中國必須產生其自己之政治家。我相信中國最大之需要不是技術，而是德行、忠心與勇氣。中國工程師已在艱難中創立鉅業，將來必更能發展。惟中國是否能解決其政治問題，乃較爲基本與令人焦慮之事實。

中國古代文化傳統已因中國以外世界之發現而破壞，但生活的新道德與新方法則尚未出現。中國實需要體會各種真理之共通性與吸收新知，以建立能作世界公民之適宜基礎，今日之學生殊極度缺乏此種哲學。

保存中國古典之德性，並加上美國之科學，尚不能認爲盡善盡美。中國於其新有之世界關係中，必須將其所有的一切生活方式重新估價。改革社會實較改良物質需要更多之智慧與耐心。推而言之，即政治學者與社會工作者更較物理學家與專家與專門技術人員爲基

一個美國朋友給中國的一封信

本。此言文學院更較工學院爲重要。或者吾人可云工程師需要品德與人性之了解，亦如其需要工程之能力一樣。派遣學生出國，應使研究人文科學者與應用科學相等。

美國與歐洲之友人，均願在中國建立與支持若干大學，中國實享受罕有之利益，此等基督教大學對於國際之了解與精神價值之貢獻，應受中國之歡迎與獎勵。我希望美國朋友如要繼續辦理此等大學，則必須在實質上提高其標準，吾人應派遣國內最優良之教師與中國，並對中國交換之教師與學生，儘量協助彼等能自由旅行於我國。此等大學應聯繫中西之最佳大學，絕無人能說此等學校於中國並不適合，其他之大學，或可聽其訓練品質不佳之學生，而教會學校則應於智識充分與社會道德兩方，皆保持其最高之水準。

教育由兩部份構成，其一爲吾人所稱之學位，另一則不易加以界說與講授，卽人格之陶冶與品德之發展，中國大多數之大學，均未注意其學生在教室以外之生活，偉大之學校，需要偉大之教授，中國顯著需要者爲品德、忠心與勇氣。

此次戰爭乃一全面戰爭，教育必須提供其對於勝利之特殊貢獻。今日已非大學保持其常態之時，筆者前面所述也不過是常態情形。現時各大國中，僅有中國之男性大學生，尚在仍然學習其所歡喜之事物。若彼等與另外一大陸上年紀相若之人相比，其感覺當爲如何？美國學生已必須離開渠等之大學生活，遠來中國，肩護保衛中國之責任、中國學生實亦應無暇留學也。

中國如欲獲得其自己之勝利，實必須訓練成千成萬之軍事專家，飛行員，無線電收發員，砲兵軍官，聯絡官，工程師，以及行政人員……等，中國大學應立即爲戰爭工作，中國或許也願意美國軍隊走入大學圈內，運送外國教師與設備，以訓練大學生爲軍隊服務，如吾人在美國所作的一樣。

一九四四年五月佳日寫於峨山

第三卷

葛德石在中国考察的报告档案

1944年
驳葛德石致中国人民书

CONFIDENTIAL

A Reply to An Open Letter Written By An American Friend of China.

By a Chinese Citizen

Dear Sir:

I read your letter with deep interest and great pleasure. As a Chinese citizen I must thank you from the bottom of my heart not only for your valuable suggestions, friendly remarks and honest and sincere critisims, but also for your spirit of comradeship and friendliness both as a friend and as an ally which so characterize the whole letter. Above all, I and every other patriotic citizens of China are very grateful to you because you have expressed, so eloquently the very feeling and thought which lie in the depth of their hearts for many years that none of us could possibly do it so well even if we were allowed to express freely. I agree with you on every main point that were mentioned in your letter, but as regards to details there may be some difference of opinion, undoubtly arised from the difference of culture and also through the different angles we are looking at the problem. Since the points you discussed in your letter are of utmost importance to us now and after the war, so I felt it is my duty as a Chinese as well as a world citizen to write you a relpy. What I am going to say below does not represent the viewpoint of the 450 millions, perhaps not even a tiny fraction of them, but all I can say is, such feelings and opinions do exist, here and there, among the people.

THE WAR PROBLEM

How to win the war ? There is no question which is more important and urgent than this one. This is a total war and the only way to win a total war is by total mobilisation of our national resources, technique and man-power. But unfortunately total mobilization in our country is only paper work. This is not the fault of the farmers and workers, because they have bore the brunt of the war for seven years. They died like ants and they died even without knowing what for! Thousands and thousands of them died of hunger, cold and disease and they never had the chance to meet the enemy in the front, nor do they have the

2.

the privelige to lodge a protest. You cannot put the blame e entirely on the intelligensia because many of them are only to glad to join the army and to defend the country. As a matter of fact, ~~mayn~~ many of our professors and students have joined the ~~people's~~-army and the guerillas as soon as the war broke out. You said in your letter that our army and government do not always welcome help and co-operation from foreigners,this is ,perhaps,true,but this does not only apply to foreigners,it also applies to our own intelligensia as well. Only recently the students are encouraged to join the army and the choice is limited to the members of the San Min Chu I youth Corps The reason is obvious. Our army is an inarticulate and illiterate army,once a large group of students joined the army then it would become articulate. An intelligent and articulate army wont tolerate corruption,bribery,blind obedience and disloyalty to their country. This perhaps can be applied to many other fields. As long as eight years ago many of us had advocated for turning the universities,colleges and middle schools into military training camps just as you are doing now in America, but our politicians have different opinions. They maintain that we need many university students for future reconstruction and planning.Our reply: a coolie army cannot win a scientific war ~~and~~ against Japan and if we were defeated then what is the use to store so many college students ? We receive no reply and we see no action ,and the war is dragged on as leisurely and as inefficiently as the warlords days. If we are too inquisitive and too energetic we may land ~~us~~ ourselves in some concentration camps.

War is won by attack and offensive but not by waiting and defensive. Our weapons are inadequate for staging big offensives, ~~and perhaps seven years of war have disappointed many~~--this is an estabblished fact,but it is also true that a peasant army cannot handle tanks,aeroplanes,big guns and battleships that ~~were~~ are given to them. It would be too cruel to say that our army had done no fighting at all,on the contrary, many divisions have fought to the last man. Our war of resistance is a heroic one but unforturatly naked heroism without the armor of tanks and

aero

3.

aeroplanes cannot win the modern war. So the only way to win a quick war ~~over~~ against Japan is to use our man power plus your weapons and techique, or the combination of ~~u~~ our infantry and your mechanized forces. We are willing to die for our country and we are happy to die for our friend and ally. It also sounds a little bit of harsh to say that we prefer waiting for the victory. As a matter ~~a~~ of fact our enemy can wait, while ~~as~~ an isolated China cannot afford to wait. We are just as earger to go back to our homes in eastern China as your soldiers would like to go back home to America. If we had the necessary weapon, technique and training we would certainly started the offensive a long time ago. To win the war outright is much cheaper than to wait for any ally. So far as I can see the following conditions must be fulfilled before we could win the war:

a. Total mobilisatiion and compulsory military service for all.

b. To raise the material as well as the cultural ~~comfort~~ standard of the army.

c. To supply us the much needed mechanized units and air-force. (People in the past has over emphasised the need of an air force but has mentioned nothing about the tanks and the mechanized force. To win battles on land it is just as important to have tanks as to have a strong air force. This is proved to be true again and again in the battles of Europe.)

d. To stop inflation at once.

The points mentioned are closely related with our politics and government so let me concentrate our attention on these topiss for a momemt.

POLITICS AND GOVERNMENT

To say that we have a dictatorial government is just as misleading as to say we have a democratic government. Dictatorship means efficiency, blitz action and ruthless punishment for offences. ~~and state authority over-rules individuality.~~ These qualities, for good or for bad, are non-existent in our government. ~~vcir~~ Corruption, bribery, blackmail, kidnap, intimidation and concentration camps are the evils of 18th century feudualistic ~~kings and landlords. Un~~

fort

4.

kings and landlords,but unfortunately these ancient "virtues" are streamlined under the 20th century autocrate and autocrat trix under-our-own-eyes. Personal interest ,clan rivalry and party intriques are the order of the day ,consequently good men cannot survi stay and patroits hesti hesitate to join the government. Perhaps you are a little bit optimistic in saying that the dictatorary trend of our government is due to the influence of Russian and German idealogy but may I remand you that the temporary government under the our national father Sun-yat-sen was the most democratic govermment ever set up in China although the Russian influence was strongest then. Democracy will flourish and bear fruits in a country where the government is in the hands of the people and fascism,Hitlerism and Nipponism will always find their roots in countries where the governments are in the hands of a few. So-our-present-regime reflects-. Dictatorship and autocracy are inherent in the ruling class of a minority and they are the byproducts of feudulism and militarism.

Every patriotic Chinese citizen believes that civil war cann be avoided and it cann be be avoided easily as soon as we have democracy. Or it can be avoided as soon as we practice San-Min-Chu-I,not by simply talking about it. So far as the people can see it, what the communists practiced in the NW is nothing but San-Min-Chu-I and,therefore,there should be no difficulty for the different parties to reach a compromise. Without democracy we cannot only win the war,but will certainly lose the peace even if our allies win the war for us.

RECONSTRUCTION.

I agree with you that we must have a planned economy after the war. Our planned economy is certainly going to follow the model that has laid down by our National father Sun-yat-sen, that is,the principles of Min-Sun-Chu-I. Local self sufficiency is narrow nationalism and imcompatible with internationism which is valued by every Chinese citizen.

As you said it we need industrialisation,we need it not only because it will give us railroads,aeroplanes,ships and a thosand other things,we need it because it will change our whole outlook of life,changes our social habits ~~of life~~,raise our material and cultural standatd of living and ~~eh~~ increase our efficiency. Fatalism is the product of an agronomy economy, lack of co-operation,the product of handicraft industry and family centred psychology the child of feudualism and primitive means of production. Above all,industralisation will cure over-population,the worst evil of our country. World statistics have demonstrated beyond any doubt that over-population is the appendix of an agricultural population. Birth rate is highest among peasant in every country and smallest among the intelligensia and the well-to-do families. The decline of birth rate in the last fifty years in the industrialized nations of Europe and America can also be used as important argument for my case. This is obvious,because machines can always produce much more and more rapidly what we needed,~~and at~~ than the soil,and at the same time machines can furnish us with all the knowledge and means about birth control,provide diversions and amusement,and change our social habits as mentioned before. It is true that we cannot become a first class industrialized nation owing to the shortage of iron, oil and some other vital minerals,but it is also true that the possibilities of science and technology are infinite.

China will remain an agricultural country for another century but I cannot agree that she will <u>always</u> remain one, at least I hope not. I shall like to see an industrialized agriculture subordinated to an urban industry. It is true that better seeds and better management can improve the livelihood of the 400 millions,but these are not all. To me the most important,demonstrated by local surveys,is to improve the land tenure system and reduce the tax.

FOREIGN RELATIONS

If you have faith in the Chinese masses then you need not worry about the foreign policy of a people's government. The smiling Chinese farmer ~~and~~ is born an internationalist, he will always reciprocate your good will with double doses whenever he has the opportunity. A smiling and hearty Chinaman

6.

is too gentle to hurt anybody and therefore cannot become a disturber of world peace. If ever you find any sign of anti-foreignism in China you may be assured that it has its roots either in our capitalism,feudualism,or other "isms" which are hostile to democracy and internationalism.

There is ,however,one thing that may disturb the peace of the world and that is a weak and poor China. For the interest of the Chinese people and for the welfare of mankind we must make our country strong and posperous. In this kind of arduous and difficult task international co-operation is welcome by the Chinese people.

EDUCATION

I and many others believe that western science and technology are the fruits of western culture and philosophy. To pick the fruits and foresake the branches,the stems and roots of western civilisation may end in disaster. So we maintain that western science and technology cannot be transplanted on the old trunks of our philosophy. Western science and technology can ~~only~~ find their roots in Chinese soil only when we have digested western culture. This means to say social sciences and philosophies of Europe and American should occupy a more important place in our universities. Our old culture and virtues are worthy of a great race and we certainly will try our best to perserve them,but this does not mean that we have to worshiped them blindly,on the contrary, we shall try to preserve what is worth preserving and try to reevaluate them in terms of 20th century landscape. Chinese renaissance has celebrated its 25th birthday this year,in the face of reactions this flood of enlightment continues to gain momentum. You need not to wait for long to witness the final struggle between the dark forces and the majestic ~~cascade~~ avanlanche of the forces of democracy.

May I also remind you that our professors and students have protested repeatedly against regimentation ~~and~~ standardization and state interference. At the same time we demanded academic freedom. The struggle is still going on and will gon on until we win the day. We want to ~~train~~ eduaate a nation of

7.

masters but not to train a horde of slaves.

Citizens of China welcome first class Christian universities. As far as education is concerned we have no fear of too much good education. Although there are many shortcomings of Christian colleges and universities there are also many good qualities. They have at least turned out a couple of conscientious,hardworking,resourceful,and responsible leaders and have built dozens of men of character. For this reason alone, if not for many other reasons,we should welcome them.

As for sending large number of students abroad many of us would prefer to invite first class professors and research men and technicians to come over to our country to teach. This is not only cheaper but also more fundamental,.The permanent centres so established will be of everlasting value to China.

Self-criticism is a virtue and this is the only excuse why I am so critical. I love my people and I also love truth,this is,perhaps,why I have written you a reply.

Forgive me for my bad English and vague ideas for this letter is written in a great hurry and amidst the cries of innocent children.

June 14th 1944.

1944年
中美文化项目建议书

Memorandum from George B. Cressey
Cultural Relations Program, Chungking

April 12, 1944

SUBJECT Preliminary Recommendations

ABSTRACT The continuation of Chinese good will is of diplomatic significance to the United States. China's universities have been of importance in this regard, and are urgently in need of literature and teaching inspiration. The recommendations deal with a) visiting Professors, b) Technical Specialists, c) Reading matter, d) Newsletters, e) Microfilm, f) Guidance to Chinese students in America, g) Chinese Professors in America, h) Chinese students in America, i) Cooperation with American agencies.

SOURCE OF DATA This report is based on five months of travel in Free China covering every major city south of the Yangtze from Kunming to Foochow, against a background of twenty years of China contacts. I have visited twenty universities and seen about as many research institutions; and have also inspected a large number of mines and factories.

My primary objective has been to bring the greetings of American scholars and to contribute to the intellectual needs of the universities, especially as an appreciation of global geography bears upon China's place in the war and peace. I have also been concerned with problems of transportation, land use, resources, reconstruction, and international relations.

I have had conversations with a large variety of people: faculty and students, officials and business men, and American residents and military personnel. In some cases I have been officially entertained and provided with transportation, in others I have lived in whatever accommodations were available and travelled by truck or bus, frequently with discomfort.

MEMORANDUM

This report is preliminary and deals largely with specific items in the field of Cultural Relations. I expect to write later on the larger aspects of American policy in Asia.

1. The cultural activities of the American government should have diplomatic significance, e.g., they must contribute to our strategic program in Asia. Mission boards and philanthropic foundations may proceed from humanitarian motives but the government must act within a political frame.

The problem is not whether China of today is an effective nation. China is important in the war program, in world peace, and in trade; and hence to our own interests. In the postwar period we shall seek commerce in large

2

volume, and shall need a strong China to checkmate Japan. World peace will be endangered as long as China is weak or chaotic. All of this requires intelligent understanding and mutual good will.

2. This is THE psychological moment in Sino-American relations. Never in twenty years have I seen so much good will. These opportunities bring large responsibilities and vital consequences whether we act or not. Many influential Chinese currently have a complex; government people who see China as one of the Big Four tend to have a superiority complex, while academic people and those caught by inflation have an inferiority complex. Neither outlook is justified, but the situation calls for psychological understanding and delicate handling. China also exhibits some of the characteristics of an adolescent; she is unable to direct her own affairs but is unwilling to accept outside guidance.

The picture is both good and bad, I alternately thrill and despair.

3. I am concerned with fascist tendencies in the Chungking government, but I find the general political situation as seen from the provinces less reactionary than I had anticipated. As measured in Chinese terms, the country has a considerable degree of unity. Nowhere in the eight provinces visited have I been able to find much support for the Communists, least of all in Kiangsi and Fukien where they once were. The Kuomintang has lost the enthusiastic support of the intelligensia, but its undesirable features diminish with distance from the capital. The Generalissimo commands undivided popular loyalty, and despite extensive questioning I have found no alternative leader. Many foreigners and thoughtful Chinese fear eventual civil war, but I would describe the situation as serious rather than alarming. I believe that America's wisest policy is to strengthen the existing government so as to make revolt impossible, and at the same time to encourage the democratic elements within it.

One of my interesting discoveries is a surprising appreciation of the Minister of Education, Mr. Chen Li-fu. While university people criticize the Ministry's regimentation, they recognize the need of bringing up the level of sub-standard schools and the great problem of finance. I am still a critic of the Ministry but they must be given credit at many points. We should cooperate.

4. Chinese universities are doing very poor work. It is customary to praise them for their efforts at carrying on under refugee conditions, but the results are scarcely creditable. This is partly due to the lack of literature and equipment, partly to serious faculty and student financial difficulties, and in part related to war weariness and psychological depression. Morale is generally very low. The universities are making almost no contribution to the war, nor to "reconstruction." Some seniors are joining interpreters' schools under the Army, but I have found no war program on any campus.

This aloofness from the national emergency is unfortunate, it relates not only to China's need for skilled military personnel but also to questions of patriotism and democracy. These are probably the only universities in any large country in the world which are continuing to operate as usual.

The best academic institution which I have visited is Amoy University. Lingnan has the most intelligent group of students. Fukien Christian University has the best school spirit. Lienta University is commonly supposed to be China's leading wartime institution, for it has the most distinguished faculty but their morale is seriously affected by inflation. Faculty salaries at Lienta have but 8 per cent of their prewar purchasing power, as compared with 15 per cent elsewhere. I have not yet visited the schools at Chengtu, nor is this a list of the best institutions.

The best student discipline, faculty interest in teaching, and character-personality development is found in the American founded schools, especially where foreigners are still on the campus. I am confident that the presence of American teachers on the campus is of major value at the present time. National universities tend to have superior faculty scholarship, but they are doing inferior teaching.

The most unfortunate trend in Chinese education is the over-emphasis on the technological and applied science side of the curriculum. This appears also in the selection of students to be sent abroad. It is obvious that China needs a great number of technicians, but even more she needs wise citizens. Western culture is a unit, and China must not repeat Japan's mistake of understanding only the material half. There needs to be more emphasis on liberal education, namely the humanities, social sciences, government, and law. China can hire foreign engineers if necessary but she must produce her own statesman.

Many colleges are operating entirely without textbooks and largely without mimeographed material. Reference books are usually very limited. Some schools are teaching science without laboratories. The level of English has declined, but at almost every university I was able to address the assembly in English with acceptable understanding. One reason for poor work in colleges is the great deterioration in the Middle Schools.

5. Industry is doing very well on the technical side. The work of the engineers is one of the brightest spots in wartime China. I have visited many blast furnaces, steel mills, and chemical plants which show a sound adjustment to Chinese requirements and which represent conspicuous ingenuity in the face of extremely difficult conditions. Many of these plants are under the able direction of Dr. Wang Wen-hao and the National Resources Commission. Industry is reasonably well financed and can pay for such foreign technical aid as it may need. The Universities on the other hand have neither the funds nor the vision to bring in foreign teachers in the humanities.

6. Two major handicaps to the war effort and to normal economic life are transportation and inflation. Roads are fair but the trucks are incredibly poor. One of the major needs is automotive rehabilitation; by reboring cylinders, replacing broken springs etc., it should be possible to make one acceptable car from two old ones. Fuel is a problem but numerous substitutes for gasoline are available.

Rising costs of labor and materials have closed many factories as their customers cannot afford to pay the necessary price of the finished product. Idle steel mills might make bomb casings and cast rails.

American military necessities may make it necessary to assist with transport and finance.

7. Specific recommendations for the Division of Science, Education and Art are as follows:

A. Since Chinese universities have a large role in public opinion and national morale, and are a powerful source of good will to America, we should strengthen their position. The greatest need is a program of American Visiting Professors who would spend one semester each in different schools. Such people should be outstanding teaching personalities rather than primarily research scholars. I would recommend that we send at least six a year, and that they all be from the field of the social sciences and humanities, including law. China today needs character and integrity more than skills. This program presumes that Chinese universities will continue much as at present; even if partially diverted to the war effort the need would remain.

B. The Technical Specialists appear to be doing a good job, but I do not see why we should finance fields in which the Chinese government or industry is able to pay its own way. Their contribution to international good will, trade, or diplomatic policy seems inadequate. I would like to see this program re-evaluated.

C. A major need is library reading matter, both books and periodicals. Many college students of the present generation have never seen a single current foreign journal, the faculty are even more intellectually starved. A few decades hence these students will determine China's foreign policy, and the proper attention today may be of incalculable value tomorrow. I appreciate the problem of importing books at present, but even a few hundred pounds a month would be of significance. It is reported that the Ministry of Education has priority for 1,000 pounds of air freight a month from India via CNAC, but that this is not being used as little can be bought there. If Science, Education and Art could arrange to collect and ship material from America, it might be possible to use this means of getting books into China. Universities are now so out of touch with the West that they do not even know what or how to order.

At a minimum we should put the pony editions of Time, Newsweek, and the New York Times Overseas Weekly in fifty libraries around China. These should be distributed from the Embassy and so stamped as a gift. In addition there should be random copies of various professional journals. One copy of each of those now sent in microfilm, or at least the more important, might be sent to the Embassy and then distributed more or less at random. Thus Science might be sent one week to Lingnan, next week's copy might go to Wuhan, etc. These journals would serve as sample reading matter rather than as research reference items like microfilm.

D. The newsletters in Psychology, Geology, etc., are well received and should be continued. In addition to abstracts they might occasionally carry items about conventions, personalities, and professional news.

E. Microfilm is a mediocre success at best. I would probably continue the program, but it is little used. The reading machines are very poor, electricity is undependable or available only at night, and the Chinese have bad eyes. Eye strain and inconvenience are universal complaints. I have seen dozens of projectors but find only polite appreciation. I should prefer to see it distributed under the auspices of the Embassy as a straight American, or Anglo-American project rather than through the "front" of Mr. T. L. Yuan, whom several people do not like. I discover that several users do not know that it is a gift from the United States.

If in the future the American publication Service becomes more exclusively a war activity than it is at present, I would see no reason for continuing to channel microfilm through it, other than the personal interests of Mr. George N. Kates, with whom I have discussed the problem. In fact it then might be a handicap to associate a largely cultural project with a military one. My understanding of microfilm is that it should be largely an academic instrument of good will rather than a trading instrument for military information. Before any such change it would be necessary to make sure that the routine work could be properly handled.

F. We need a much more conscious program in America of friendly guidance and introduction to democracy for the new Chinese students and apprentices shortly to be sent abroad. Their indoctrination in the Central Training Corps and subsequent supervision while abroad needs to be considered.

No one in China knows to which institutions these students should be sent under wartime conditions, yet they must be accepted by some school before they can receive a visa. American universities are equally in the dark as to current standards in China. Students' programs may need to be considerably revised after arrival. I should personally urge that all wartime graduates of Chinese universities be required to repeat their Senior year, and possible Junior as well, at a small college in a small town of the Pomona, Carleton, Oberlin, Swarthmore, type. Chinese educational values have depreciated to half their prewar standard.

G. I am not clear as to the theory on which taxpayers' money is spent to bring Chinese professors to the United States unless there is a definite program on speaking and mutual interpretation, more than I observed a year ago. Are we succeeding in buying political good will in this way? In any case I would certainly reduce the per diem to $6. per day. The present scale will create impossible precedents for the foundations and missions who normally bring people over. Chinese universities should provide for family expenses here.

H. I see no justification for the continued support of Chinese students stranded in America. Put them to work or send them home. Nor do I see justification for the Cultural Relation movie program.

I. All of the government's cultural program with China is a continuation and extension of the century-old activities of American missionaries, foundations, and business men. Our existing contributions in the educational field have been of the greatest international significance. Thus the dozen American-founded universities such as Lingnan, Nanking, and Yenching, plus Tsinghua, have been a major source of good will. Much of the political advantage which we now enjoy, plus the trade and alliances which we seek, flow from the work of these and similar cultural enterprises.

I believe that a sound Department of State program in Science, Education and Art should recognize this situation and channel a considerable part of its activity through existing American institutions. We as a nation benefit when West China Union, Soochow, Ginling and Cheeloo Universities are strong; we equally suffer if they weaken. I therefore urge much closer cooperation with the Associated Boards in New York City.

1944年
中美文化项目小结

Memorandum from George B. Cressey
Cultural Relations Program in China

Syracuse, August 19,1944

SUBJECT Summary Observations

ABSTRACT The cultural relations program has vital diplomatic significance in war-time China. The major needs are American visiting professors and current literature.

SOURCE OF DATA This memoranda is based upon nearly a year of travel in Asia, including widespread contacts in university centers and with prominent Chinese.

1. China is an essential element in world peace and American policy
   a. The defeat of Japan, which is both a continental and maritime power, requires major operations in China.
   b. Our best safeguard for peace in the Pacific, and as a checkmate against Japan, is a strong China.
   c. The reconstruction of China offers a major market for American exporters, especially of producers goods.
   d. We seek the advancement of the democratic way of life, and it is to our advantage to have China develop along the lines of international cooperation rather than toward fascist autarchy.

2. Intelligent good will is of enormous practical diplomatic significance
   a. The succession of Chinese students who have studied in the United States, and the American missionaries who have lived in China, have provided a basis of understanding which now means that we and China are among the United Nations.
   b. The American ublic has a great amount of sentimental good will for China, and vice versa, but it lacks real understanding and is thus subject to upsets; e.g. the article by White in Life and by Drew Pearson.

3. These are critical days for China
   a. Basic decisions are in the balance between contrasting ways of life.
   b. Never has there been so much popular good will for the U.S.A. We can ake of China any kind of a country we wish, and easily, if we act intelligently.
   c. Public opinion stems from a small group of intellectuals, returned students, and universities, who are desperately starved for current ideas and spiritual support.
   d. The major need in the field of cultural relations between China and the U.S.A. is two fold: personalities and

-2-

literature. 1. One or two dozen outstanding Americans; mature personalities, good speakers, understanding teachers; can lift the morale of a university and its whole community and enable China to make a larger contribution in the war. 2. China's intellectual starvation is serious, and a few hundred pounds of books and magazines a month will do more to win the war and to save the lives of American soldiers than several times the same weight of munitions.

e. China's major needs are no so much in techniques or skills as in character, courage and loyalty. This calls for aid in the field of ideas, e.g. the humanities, social sciences, law, and democracy. Spiritual ideals and motives are basic.

4. The U.S. needs a much larger number of competent specialists on China

The war has revealed a critical shortage of linguists, geographers, economists, and all types of experienced personnel; and of those who appreciate Chinese psychology. (Army headquarters in Chungking has but one person with a China background, and Washington agencies have but a handful).

a. a wisely administrated cultural relations program, plus a more liberal training program for Foreign Service officers could build up a reserve of hundreds of Americans with China competence. These would form a reserve back log for future needs.

5. All international contacts have political significance.

The world is now so interdependent that humanitarian and commercial relations have diplomatic repercussions.

a. The Department of State must give increasing attention and support to all types of world-wide human relations. This means closer cooperation with existing foundations, missionary societies, etc. plus active supplementary activity in fields not already covered.
b. Guidance must be provided for Chinese students coming to the United States.

6. There is urgent and immediate need for American cultural representatives in China

1. The work to be done includes:
   a. intellectual interpretation of one country to another.
   b. liasion between Chinese and American universities; including guidance for students coming to the U.S.A., the evaluation of Chinese universities, and interchange of ideas and material.
   c. aid to cultural institutions, libraries, research workers and all intellectual activities.
   d. expediting war time shipments of books, magazines, and scientific equipment.
2. This is the proper field for a Cultural Attache under the Embassy, for the results have diplomatic value and must not be left to chance, and can be furthered by the use of Department of State facilities for the accumulation and transmission of materials.

-3-

On the other hand, the work of cultural relations calls for considerable initiative and freedom, both in judgment and in public address, and this may not be feasible under existing government regulations. In such case all or part of the work must be left to private agencies such as the Institute of Pacific Relations, the Rockefeller and other foundations, the Associated Boards for Christian Colleges, the Association of American Colleges, etc.

7. Specific China Recommendations for the Division of Science, Education and Art

China is not doing her full part in the war, in part because of low morale. The following recommendations have long range diplomatic importance but are presented in terms of their immediate military significance. I believe that they will save the lives of American soldiers and shorten the war.

a. We should send Visiting Professors who will spend a semester or a year at a single university. These should be rich personalities and able speakers with a mature philosophy of life. Such people can be of service in any subject or connection, e.g. as Technical Specialists attached to a ministry, but their maximum service will be in a University (possibly arranged through the Ministry of Education) and in the field of the social sciences, humanities, law, etc., rather than technology, engineering or applied science.

b. We must find some way to send literature. At present the only bulk shipment of any periodical from the outside world is 41 copies of the India edition of Time, distributed by O.W.I. to key individuals. This supply should be trebled, and supplemented by the New York Times Overseas Weekly, the pony editions of Newsweek and Life, and a few more serious journals such as Atlantic and Harpers. Key books such as Walter Lippman and Sumner Welles would be of great value.

Small shipments can be made without difficulty by Diplomatic sea pouch and by Army Post Office. Larger amounts can be flown from Calcutta to Chungking by C.N.A.C.; for example. O.W.I. has twice chartered a plane and would be glad to share space with the Division of Science, Education and Arts. If these fail, the Chinese Ministry of Education will fly the material in on their own quota.

8. Previous Memoranda

Additional suggestions may be found in the following memoranda.
Cultural Relations Objectives - December 26, 1943
Chinese Students Coming to America - January 2, 1944
Preliminary Recommendations - April 12, 1944
Cultural Imperialism - May 27, 1944
Evaluation of Chinese Universities - May 27, 1944
American Aid for Chinese Educational Needs - May 27, 1944
List of Chinese Institutions of Higher Education - June 7, 1944

1944年
中美文化关系备忘录

(C O P Y)

MEMO: SINO-AMERICAN INTELLECTUAL RELATIONS

The present war and the future reconstruction of international relations are closely related; in time of war we must prepare for peace, and the following proposals regarding intellectual relations between China and the United States are submitted for immediate consideration and action.

The intellectual relations between two countries cannot be left to chance. The United States has a carefully planned program of lend-lease and military aid to China, and both countries maintain extensive publicity programs. The export of lend-lease materials and current information, however, does not cover the whole range of international relations; such things are ephemeral and may not necessarily build a permanent basis of understanding. In addition to present programs aimed at winning the war, there is urgent need of a long-range program in the field of education and the exchange of ideas. To be effective, this program should be throughly prepared and partly initiated before peace arrives. This work cannot wait for a peace which may be long in coming.

Two principles must underlie such a program. The first is that ideas are as important as technics. American technical assistance may hasten the industrialization of China, as it did of Japan, without necessarily bringing China and the United States closer in thought and feeling. It is worth remembering that the last generation in the West was highly gratified at the "westernization" of Japan, although to us it is now clear that this "westernization" was but a means serving Japanese ends. We need not fear China's aims, but we should not delude ourselves by assuming that railroads and factories will make China into a second United States. International understanding is not to be achieved by the export of goods and services alone.

The second principle therefore is that a program of intellectual relations with China must be reciprocal. The American people have almost as much to learn about China as the Chinese have learned from them. Chinese culture has certain values to offer. More than that, China is in the American world and if the United States is to play its part properly in this new world it must understand the other actors.

The program which we propose involves two general types of activity, concerned with printed matter and with personnel, respectively. The development of intellectual relations cannot be blue-printed in advance, but several lines of action can now be laid down, without any doubt as to their permanent value.

1

- 2 -

1. Libraries: It goes without saying that collections must be built continuously, and it is high time for action both in China and in the United States. The current purchasing program and an editing and publishing program of the National Library of Peiping are attached (see enclosure). Plans must now be made for the creation or supplementing of at least a score of libraries of western books in China, together with files of western periodicals. The collection of these periodical files calls for the immediate attention of the American Library Association Committee on Aid to Libraries in War Areas (Dr. Wayne M. Hartwell, Rush Rhees Library, University of Rochester)

A-B

C

In the United States Chinese collections of some sort now exist at the following places: the Library of Congress, Harvard, Yale, Columbia, Princeton, Pennsylvania, Duke, Cornell, Chicago, Michigan, Colorado, California, Claremont Colleges, College of Chinese Studies, and the University of Washington, to name only well-known centers. Whatever may be the quality of these collections now, it is not too much to expect that twenty American institutions will develop Chinese libraries of a general nature after the war. When to this number are added libraries in Canada, Great Britain, and on the Continent, it is plain that a large future demand may be expected, not only for books published in Free China during the war but also for newspaper and periodical files.

D

To meet this demand the undersigned, Library of Congress representative in China, proposes that the Library of Congress act as a central agency and immediately undertake a program in China in cooperation with the National Library of Peiping along the following lines: (1) microfilming of back files of leading Chungking newspapers, particularly the Ta Kung Pao, Hsin Hua Jih Pao, and Chung Yang Jih Pao, now combined with the Sao Tang Pao. (2) purchase or collection of five copies of governmental and institutional publications, for storage with the American Embassy in Chungking until transportation is arranged. (3) purchase and storage of files of other periodicals and of current books on a selective basis. (The collection of five copies is proposed under (2) because current Chinese publications, owing to the scarcity of paper and costs of printing, are in limited editions and may soon be out of print).

E

This program has been begun; but costs are high in China and steadily mounting: an extensive investment is required, which may run to 20,000 in 1943. Unless the Library of Congress is prepared to foot the bill it is essential that someone in the United States, presumably the Library of Congress, immediately undertake to coordinate the requests and canalize the funds of American libraries which may be interested. Action is therefore solicited on the part of the library authorities in Washington.

2. Publications: The supply of printed matter necessarily involves the preparation of bibliographical

guides.

- 3 -

guides. As one such help to western students of China, the Quarterly Bulletin of Chinese Bibliography has met a
F favorable response, and its continuation in March 1943 is now planned by the National Library of Peiping with the assistance of the Sino-American Cultural Institute,
G Chungking. We suggest that the American Council of Learned Societies, or a similar body, undertake the reprinting of a photoduplicated edition in the United States, and the response of Dr. Mortimer Graves is solicited on this point.

Consideration has also been given in China to the publication in the United States of certain journals like the Nankai Social and Economic Quarterly or T'ien Hsia Monthly. It is conceivable that the editors of the
H Far Eastern Quarterly might well lend their covers temporarily to the text of a sister Chinese journal in English such as the Nankai Quarterly, as a gesture of scholarly solidarity. This particular possibility should be called to the attention of Dr. C. H. Peake and Dr. H. D. Fong.

In China the most pressing intellectual need at this moment is for western publications, and this need is being partly met by the supplying, under the Cultural Relations Program of the Department of State, of American learned journals on microfilm. In order to make these microfilm
I materials better known, a mimeographed catalog is now distributed by the Chinese committee in charge of their use, which is known as the International Cultural Service of China; and it is further proposed to compile a mimeo-
J graphed Microfilm Digest which will indicate tables of contents and include comments on important materials available in the microfilm libraries which have been or soon will be established in Chungking, Shapingpa (the nearby university center), Chengtu, Kunming.

Bibliographical publications such as the above, always adapted to the needs of the moment, are a constant necessity for the development of international studies and should be constantly facilitated. Directories of personnel are equally needed. The National Library of Peiping proposes to compile
K a Who's Who of American Returned Students in China, indicating the competence of each person. In a world where technical training is at a premium, this will have obvious interest both for the Chinese and for the American governments.

3. Training of personnel is now of greater importance to the United States than the building of libraries, because it has been allowed to lag behind. The existence in the United States of more than one Chinese library containing over 100,000 volumes, in places where serious users of such a library number less than a dozen persons day by day, is evidence of this fact. Ideas are exchanged both by books and by persons, and both must be provided in larger quantities. It can also be done by private agencies, as has been the custom heretofore, and we urge that the
L Harvard-Yenching Institute and the Rockefeller Foundation in particular consider the granting of fellowships for study in China at the post-graduate level beginning in the autumn 1943, especially in economics. Transportation and semi-official status for such research students should be arranged

with the cooperation of federal agencies such as the Research and Analysis Branch of the Office of Strategic
M Services, who are in dire need of trained personnel. We express the hope that such cooperation can be inaugurated. In China such students could work in a great variety of institutions, both governmental and private.

American technical experts in many lines of scientific work are now being sent to China by the Cultural Relations Division and will be of great usefulness. It is worth noting, however, that none of these experts is concerned with the humanities and few even with social science. They are not meant to be communicators of general ideas, and the Division should
N therefore be urged by interested citizens to consider a further program along the lines now being followed by the British, who are sending a Regius Professor Greek, not for his technical ability but because he is an outstanding individual in the academic world.

At present a number of Chinese students are being trained in the United States; the Cultural Relations program of the Department of State is partly directed to this end, and students are being sent by the National Resources Commission and other Chinese government agencies. This activity is largely at the technological level, in response to the Chinese need for technical personnel. But it is plainly in the interest of cultural understanding that the humanities and social studies play some part; and we urge that an interim program of scholarships for this
O purpose be considered by the Division of Humanities of the Rockefeller Foundation and by the Harvard-Yenching Institute. The undersigned are ready to take responsibility for the formation of a small committee of selection in China,
P the membership of which would be previously approved in the United States, and which would pick out a dozen or twenty of the most promising Chinese research students for further training in the United States in 1943. The transportation of such students can be arranged by air to India and by ship thereafter. This would be a means both of training and of preserving as scholars young men of proved ability and scholarly bent who may otherwise be forced by the extreme pressure of circumstance to give up their careers.

In present circumstances the preservation of Chinese scholarly personnel, by a system of grants-in-aid of research, is as necessary as the training of new scholars. We urge that both the Rockefeller Foundation and the
Q Harvard-Yenching Institute consider a program of grants for research, to be administered partly by a committee in China, for the purpose of securing the completion of research work now in progress in the field of Chinese studies and on the part of scholars who do not require study abroad. The sending of Chinese professors to lecture in the United States, which has been inaugurated by the Cultural Relations Division, should be supplemented by grants for use in China. We suggest that direct grants by private agencies to carefully selected recipients are the most effective means of preserving Chinese scholarship in wartime without the delays and complications which inhibit official programs.

We

- 5 -

We submit that action should be taken at this time by private as well as by government agencies. For example, it is highly desirable to train Chinese library and museum personnel by interneships in the United States as preparation for the rebuilding of Chinese institutions, yet it is difficult to give such training a high official priority in war-time, in spite of its fundamental importance. There are many such fields in which unofficial support should supplement official action.

4. An American Institute in China is urgently needed to guide and encourage the manifold development of intellectual relations between the United States and China. Like the
R China Institute in America, this agency should have an official character and yet be quite separate and distinct from the Embassy and diplomatic channels. From the variety of the projects mentioned above, to which many more could be added, it is evident that some measure of coordination will be necessary in the near future. This coordination of Sino-American intellectual relations should be undertaken by a small office in the Chinese capital which would act as a clearing-house and a source of stimulation and advice, rather than as an originator of large projects. An official character is required to give it a sanction for coordinating work, but an extensive use of federal funds may be less desirable than a variety of private enterprises, to which the American Institute in China could lend invaluable assistance.

This new office might act for the Library of Congress and for the Cultural Relations Division in certain respects, and it might take over certain residual activities left by the Office of War Information and the Interdepartmental Committee for the Acquisition of Foreign Publications. It might also be able to put some of the activities of the Sino-American Cultural Institute in Chungking on a sounder basis. By integrating projects which now overlap or lack proper coordination, it could be a measure of economy.

This new office will be especially needed to inaugurate an extensive program of student and teacher exchanges, similar to that supervised so successfully by the Institute of Inter-
S national Education between the United States and countries to the east and south. The rebuilding of Chinese educational institutions after the war may be expected to create a great number of campuses where American teachers and students can live and work with profit. While exchanges should no doubt be set up between institutions directly, an official supervisory agency will be needed and will have much to do.

In order to achieve a meeting of minds at this distance, the readers of this memorandum are asked to reply to it, even if briefly, paragraph by paragraph, and to transmit their replies if no better means offers through Dr. F.G. Kilgour, Interdepartmental Committee, Bldg. 14, 25th and E Streets N.W., Wash., D.C. The undersigned propose to go ahead with the projects above marked A,B,C,F,I,J,and K. Action from you is expected on the other subjects.

Respectfully

- 6 -

Respectfully submitted,

(Signed) T. L. YUAN

T. L. Yuan
Director, National Library of Peiping,
Executive Secretary, International Cultural
Service of China.

(Signed) J. K. FAIRBANK

J. K. Fairbank
Far Eastern Representative,
Library of Congress
China Director, Interdepartmental Committee
for the Acquisition of Foreign Publications.

December 31, 1942

copies to Messrs: David H. Stevens, S. Elisseeff, Mortimer Graves, A. W. Hummel, Lauchlin Currie, Roger S. Greene, C.F.Remer, Chih Meng, W.W.Lockwood, Mme. Wilma Fairbank.

第四章（1945–1950）

1945年，葛德石返回美国之后，根据在中国的切身体验以及他的专业素养，他以一个地理学家的身份对公众阐述了自己对中美关系的看法，以期中美友好。同时在专业领域，葛德石发表自己对中国地理研究的最新报告。1950年，葛德石计划再次前来中国进行地理考察，并制定了详细的规划，可惜最终未能如愿成行。

1945年
葛德石关于中美关系的广播讲话稿

1945 年，葛德石返回美国之后，根据在中国的切身体验以及他的专业素养，他以一个地理学家的身份对公众阐述了自己对中美关系的看法，以期中美友好。同时在专业领域，葛德石发表自己对中国地理研究的最新报告。1950 年，葛德石计划再次前来中国进行地理考察，并制定了详细的规划，可惜最终未能如愿成行。

Cressey-1

CHINA

The world is full of places, so many of them that for most of us they are merely spots on the map, blank areas which hold the globe together. China is more than a mere place, for here is a unique phenomenon. Other lands are older and others more beautiful but nowhere else have so many people lived for so many centuries so close to nature. On all sides the landscape reflects the intensity of man's occupation of the earth. No other country is so mature in its adjustments between man and nature. Within our lifetime this venerable land has become one of the recognized Big Five of the United Nations.

China is not only ancient, it is diverse as well. Few countries exhibit greater contrasts, and no simple generalization can do justice to all of its geography. Rainfall varies from one inch a year in the deserts to 100 inches on the coastal mountains. Extensive forests stand in contrast to denuded hill-sides. The people in the south eat rice three times a day while elsewhere it is a once-a-year luxury. In fact more people in China live on wheat than is the case in the United States. The great seaport of Shanghai is one of the cosmopolitan cities of the world, but one has only to go a few hundred yards beyond its borders to find a primitive agricultural countryside.

Even greater than these visible differences are the invisible contrasts within peoples minds. If we could only use a mental x-ray, I am sure that we would be amazed over the

Cressey-2

confusion between the old and the new; the contrasts between classical superstition and modern ideas.

China is big, larger than the United States by a million square miles. China is old, older than the United States by three thousand years. China is populous, with four times the population of the United States. All these give her an inertia which is not easily redirected. Physicists tell us that momentum is mass times velocity. China's present economic "velocity" is low, but her mass is very great. She has not shown the quick adjustability which has characterized the more compact land of Japan, but the power is there. Let me put it this way. Japan is like a Ford V8, notable for its quick acceleration and flashy performance. China is a ten ton truck, which takes longer to get under way. But if it comes to a collision, I would rather be riding in the truck.

Within the vast expanse of greater China there has grown up over the centuries a civilization which, while different from ours, nevertheless has many points of similarity. The Chinese have a fundamental social democracy and a practical approach to the problems of life which at once command our respect. Here is none of the mysticism of India, nor the deceptiveness of the Japanese. We find them to be a likeable people, and the amount of good will which they have for our country is very impressive.

I need not tell you that these are difficult days for China, probably the most critical for many decades. The problem for us, however, is not whether the China of 1945 is good or bad but whether China is important. That, I believe she is, not only as an ally in our common task of ~~defeating~~ controlling Japan, but as a partner in the creation of a peaceful world with expanding trade and closer cultural contacts. // Twice before in our history we have found that the China trade was a major factor in our internal prosperity. Just as our commerce with China after the Revolutionary War and the War of 1812 helped to put our early nation on its feet economically, so it is again possible that trade with Asia may be of great significance in the days immediately ahead. China, too, holds the key to peace in the Pacific for if we can assist in the creation of a strong democratic China as an American ally, we need not again fear trouble with Japan.

We now recognize China as one of the five great powers, not as a power in being but as a nation whose economic and cultural potentials are of great significance. China moves slowly and it may be a decade or more before she has fully put her house in order, but I am confident that within our lifetimes we shall find China to be a power in being as well as a powerful nation in her potentials.

The Chinese are a nation of farmers, and it is from the soil that the products of their culture have come. So true is this that China has been described as having a vegetable civilization. There are few other places on earth where the same soil has yielded so many harvests. Literally trillions

For at least 30 centuries the farmers have tilled the same fields

Cressey-4

of people have lived on this good earth. But unfortunately the good earth is not always good. Nor is there enough of it.

Here is one of the basic problems in China: too many people on not enough land. I do not mean that greater China is not large enough, the problem is the very limited extent of arable land in the areas where people live. Vast deserts and towering mountains occupy too large a fraction.

In all of China the cultivated land, that is to say the land actually producing crops, amounts to some 300,000 square miles (remember that figure of 300,000). In contrast, we in America have 500,000 square miles of crop land with which to support one-fourth China's population. But whereas we might greatly enlarge our 500,000 square miles now under cultivation, the Chinese find it economically impossible to increase their 300,000 square miles. If we put it in terms of the individual, each man, woman, and child in China must obtain his livelihood from less than half an acre of productive soil, whereas in this country the figure is eight times as large, or 2.5 acres per capita. With an expanding population and a limited agricultural acreage, China faces one of her major problems.

China has three great geographic assets. These are coal, man power and location. In coal, China ranks fourth among all the nations with vast reserves of high grade fuels. Here is the key to industrial power. Unfortunately many people have assumed that an abundance of coal implied an abundance of other mineral resources as well. The fact is that, Despite widespread misinformation, China is not a fabulously rich country in her metallic resources, such as iron or copper, but no other nation in eastern Asia is so well endowed. While the reserves are modest they are adequate

If I may give you another set of figures, you may like to know how China's coal reserves compare with ours. The picture is this. In all the world the known coal supply amounts to about 7 trillion tons. Of this unimaginable total we in the U.S. have 3 1/2 trillion or over 1/2. The Soviet Union comes second, followed by Canada. China is a poor fourth but her reserves will last for centuries.

Cressey-5

for some decades to come. Within a decade after the return of peace, we shall doubtless see something of the same spectacular industrialization which characterized the Soviet Union during its five year plans. China may always remain fundamentally an agrarian country, but large scale industry will develop in a few favorable areas.

China's millions provide the world's largest source of labor. At present they are inefficient but there is no reason why two generations of training may not make labor as skilled as in Europe. A limited diet and a somewhat too warm climate are handicaps, but the sheer bulk of China's man power is impressive. The new China will have an enormous amount of work to be done in building roads, controlling rivers, improving agriculture and operating factories. The people to do the job are available.

Location is an important geographic resource, since the possession of material assets is of little value in Antarctica or Central Africa. No other nation in eastern Asia enjoys China's locational advantages, except perhaps Japan which we may well eliminate for the immediate future. China dominates the trade and strategy of the western Pacific.

China emerges from the second World War as the weakest of the Big Five of the United Nations, but with very large resources. Before the end of the Twentieth Century she will probably have caught up with the west and regained her historic leadership in the east. In this new ~~global~~ age of the air age, we need to look at the globe + relearn our geography. Whereas we once spoke of China as lying

Cressey-6

in the Far East, we now recognize that China is our new neighbor across the Pacific in the Near West. Or to put it more properly, China is our new neighbor to the north, for the shortest route from this country to China lies northward over the Arctic. With the return of peace, we shall be able to fly from New York to Shanghai as quickly as we ~~may~~ now travel by rail from New York to San Francisco. In such a small world we do well to understand the ~~problems~~ geography of our neighbors, one of the most important of whom will surely come to be the new China.

1947年
葛德石关于中国景观的报告

PRINCETON UNIVERSITY
BICENTENNIAL CONFERENCE ON
FAR EASTERN CULTURE AND SOCIETY
April 1-3, 1947

THE CHINESE LANDSCAPE

by George B. Cressey

ACCESSIBILITY

Ancient China was like a huge oasis. On all sides there were barriers which handicapped intercourse with the outside world. Tropical jungles, towering mountains, broad deserts, and the widest of oceans united to preserve the unity and isolation of China. Small wonder that the country became self-centered.

Southeastern Asia is isolated by nature on all sides except the north. Against the nomads of the desert Chin Shih Huang-ti built the Great Wall in an effort to perfect China's oasis-like isolation. The Wall was an attempt to define the boundary between the wandering nomad of the steppe and the settled farmer of the humid agricultural lands to the south. This attempt to fix a shifting climatic boundary was doomed to failure, for deserts expand and contract. If the Great Wall were to have succeeded, it should have been placed on skids and moved back and forth with changing rainfall cycles.

The most significant geographic fact in China's modern history is her new relation to the ocean. Formerly China faced to the north and west, and the Pacific was the back door. The Jade Gate near the end of the Great Wall in Kansu was the front entrance, and contacts with Inner Asia played a dominant role in the history of the country. It was the steppe dwellers of Mongolia, Manchuria, and Tibet who repeatedly invaded China, rather than peoples from across the empty ocean.

Today this has changed. China has turned about face and now fronts on the Pacific. Shanghai and Canton have replaced Lanchow and Kalgan as China's front doors. The ocean is now a great highway over which has come trade and knowledge. Even more important than the things which China imports are the ideas which have come across the ocean. China's most important neighbors are no longer in the interior of Asia but lie in the four corners of the world. The bewildering social and economic revolution which is rushing China onward is largely due to her new accessibility. Shanghai is today the main entrance to China, and the Jade Gate but a poetic memory.

MATURITY

China is a land where man lives very close to nature. Centuries of crowded occupance have brought livelihood into intimate adjustment with the environment. Whereve one travels, people have pressed on the land to the limit of its capacity. The roots of the Chinese truly go deep into the earth. Unfortunately this earth is not always good.

The most significant element in the geographic landscape is thus not topography or rainfall or vegetation, but man and his words. One cannot escape from the ever-present people. They are as much a part of nature as the hills themselves. Here is an organic unity in which man and the environment are bound together as intimately as a tree and its soil. So truly is man a part of the environment that the physical and cultural landscape is blended into a common whole.

George B. Cressey - 2 -

Long ago the Chinese came to use their resources up to the limits of their technological skills. Modern engineering may reclaim waste lands or develop new mines and add transport facilities, but until China discovered western skills she had developed a mature stabilized material culture. In ecological terms, China represented a climax formation.

Many elements of geography are constant, but others change. Climate moves in a complex system of cycles. Topographic erosion leads to floods and river changes. Soils and minerals become depleted. Even more significant are the developments which follow from the availability of new skills. The geographic influences which bear upon Chinese society today are not all the same as in the past. Isolation has given way to access. Flood and drought gradually yield to river control and irrigation. Populations increase and distribution patterns shift. Previously unknown minerals lead to modern industry. Despite these changes the basic factors of configuration, rainfall, and position remain. It is still true that China is rooted in the earth. So long as so many people live on so little good land, the Chinese will continue to have intimate contacts with the earth. Man cannot escape his geography for he is a part of it.

REGIONAL DIVERSITY

No land on earth has greater regional contrasts in topography, or climate, or crops. Here is the world's greatest plateau, its driest desert, its most diversified agriculture. The island of Hainan is within 18 degrees of the Equator, northern Manchuria is but 13 degrees from the Arctic Circle. Temperature extremes from north to south are greater than along a comparable stretch of our Atlantic seaboard.

Population densities are equally varied, from the emptiness of the Taklamakan Desert to the congestion of the Yangtze delta. No map of China is more meaningful than one of population, for it states a fact and presents a challenge. Such a map is at the same time automatically a representation of where people live, a map of agricultural land, and a map of arable potential; change the legend and the same map will serve. Those who see in the uneven spread of China's population merely a need for better transportation and resettlement fail to appreciate how little of China's land is suitable for occupance.

Within China are three large geographic super regions or provinces, the dry North, the humid South, and the empty interior. North China is a land of limited and uncertain precipitation, with but four to six months' growing season, and for much the year a brown landscape. South China, in contrast, has abundant and dependable rainfall, nine to twelve months' growing season, and a characteristic greeness. The north is influenced by the desert, the south is maritime. Out of these climatic differences have come major contrasts in land use and agricultural prosperity. The soils of North China are unleached, and ill suited to rice, while South China has leached soils. In technical terms, these are pedocals and pedalfers. Perhaps the simplest terms by which to characterize provinces is to call the north the wheat area, and the south the rice area.

These contrasts are not only material, they are human as well. The people of Shangung average 2 ½ inches taller than those of Canton. This is presumably not a matter of climatic selection, but rather of intermixture with Mongolian and Manchu invaders. All those familiar with China will recognize further regional contrasts in temperatment and culture.

All of this points to problems of economic and political coherence. China is compact, but it is also diverse. Geographic fractionalization is a major difficulty in any program of unification. If China is to have a coherent government, one of the first problems is the development of transportation and the breakdown of excessive regionalism.

LAND AND PEOPLE

No problem in China is more pressing than the combination of so many people on so little land. Although China has nearly four times the population of the United States, cultivated land amounts to but four-fifths that in America. In the United States some 570,000 square miles of land are plowed for crops,inn China the corresponding figure is no greater than 425,000. What is more, the United States, if pressed, might almost double its acreage, while China cannot increase its crop land by more than a very nominal figure, say 5 per cent.

China has less than half an acre of food-producing land per person. From this must come his food, shelter, clothing, and taxes. Where 1485 people must live on each square mile of cultivated soil, theee cannot be much more than enough income to keep body and soul together. In some areas, the farm density is even twice this figure.

The Chinese farmer is properly to be praised for his painstaking skill in securing good yields from soil which has grown as many as 7000 harvests. The test of agriculture, however, is not the yield per acre but the yield per person. Where we in the United States grow an acre of wheat with 1.2 days labor, China requires 26 days. In corn, the comparison is 2.5 to 23, even in cotton the difference is 14 days per acre in America and 56 days on China. In total yield per farmer, the American farmer produced 14 times as much as his Chinese competitorl

Since China's population cannot be reduced, or substantially redistributed, and since cultivated land cannot be materially increased, the principal hope is in better soils and fertilizer, and in better farm management.

Even if China had major opportunities for industrialization, which does not appear probable, there is no surplus food on the farms with which to feed an enlarged urban population.

Improved transportation, flood control and agricultural management may remove the threat of famine, but if the Chinese are to take their place as prosperous citizens of the United Nations, there is no more important problem that the relations between land and people.

1950年
葛德石中国地理考察计划

I. Program

This is a major program of geographic research in China, with five facets. The project concerns an evaluation of China's prospects and potentials during the academic year 1950-51. To a considerable extent these projects are the continuation of work already under way.

1. The most conspicuous result will be a book similar to "China's Geographic Foundations". This is now the only systematic volume in English on Chinese geography, and has had wide use as a text and by the general reader. Its value to China is attested by at least three pirated editions. It is appropriate to point out that this book was made possible by C.S.R.C. grants of $1,600. and $500. in 1929-31; plus about $1,250. from the Institute of Pacific Relations.

2. As a basis for valid generalization, I plan to prepare two or three detailed studies, similar to my monographs on the Ordos and Chekiang. Political conditions at the time will determine their location and character, but the projects in mind include settlement possibilities in the northwest, the topographic basis for agriculture in some southern province, transportation needs in terms of natural resources and markets, and problems of livelihood and population in small representative areas such as my Fenghsien study. While these studies would be classed as human geography, my geologic interests should enable me to provide a solid physical basis for evaluation.

3. Both of the above require field work as well as office analysis of statistics and other material in Chinese. I have already visited all of China's 28 provinces, plus Outer Mongolia. During the year I hope to travel widely in order to observe recent changes, collect new material, and verify regional boundaries. It will be exceedingly worth while if we can take along our car.

4. I am genuinely anxious to serve my Chinese colleagues. While I do not wish to settle down in any one school as Visiting Professor, I certainly hope to lecture in several Departments of Geography, both large and small. I carry on an active correspondence with many Chinese geographers and believe that I can make a substantial contribution in person. I regard this contribution to the morale and professional growth of Chinese geographers as a particular service.

5. The United States is very poorly supplied with geographers who know China. This is a matter of national concern, and of obvious importance in academic Area Programs. Under current conditions it is difficult for this generation of graduate students to undertake satisfactory field work alone. One of the important parts of my program is to take along half a dozen advanced students for field training. Most would work on dissertations. I am already preparing three such people and am anxious for early decisions in order to select the others prior to next winter. Their selection is obviously a joint matter. I recognize the responsibility of this field-seminar training, but regard it as one of the major contributions which I can make.

George B. Cressey - 2

II. **Plans**

I propose to spend the academic year 1950-51 in China. My application for a Fullbright grant has been submitted to Dr. Gordon Bowles. If unsuccessful I shall apply elsewhere including the S.S.R.C. No other requests are pending. Preparations have been under way for a year and I have formal invitations from the University of Nanking, the Department of Geography at National Central University, and the China Institute of Geography (of which I am an Honorary Fellow).

These may seem inauspicious times to work in China, but my experience of 25 years has shown that there are always some parts of the country where worth while work is possible. I am convinced of the growing gravity of China's problems, and of the necessity for a fuller understanding of the geographic fundamentals.

It is an essential part of the program that I take along our family. In addition to Mrs. Cressey this means our four children, ages 13 to 23. It is obvious that we would not wish to be separated, but it is also true that I regard our contribution as a family to be an important part of the program, both in service to Chinese geographers and to the half dozen American students who are a part of the project. I may add that Mrs. Cressey has lived in China, and that we have many friends there.

My present travel intentions are about as follows. The initial objective would be Nanking, if still the capital and educational center. Here we would hope to find a house which would serve as headquarters for the year. After a month or two there, I would spend a few weeks each in Peiping and Canton. This should develop the necessary contacts and make me familiar with recent data. Then might follow a month each in a couple of areas for local field studies plus visits to university departments. Following these travel experiences I would return to Nanking for several solid months of research and writing. Brief but extensive travel for checking purposes might follow. I would hope to have the bulk of the manuscript for the new book well in hand before leaving China.

I fully recognize that the total program will be unusually costly, particularly as it relates to transportation. I can only reply that I anticipate worth while benefits from each expenditure. Costs for our family will be a major item but I feel that we can thus better serve China. I have had to leave them behind on several other occasions and do not feel it fair to do so this time. The student project should yield material results. Here is another specific reason for taking along Mrs. Cressey and our family; without a home of our own as a base the project might involve too many personal hazards. I assume that you recognize unique values in contributions from senior scholars, and it is inevitable that more money is required.

It would be my guess that China will have found some solution for her political problems by 1950. Short of complete chaos, I am prepared to go ahead, alone if absolutely necessary. We cannot wait indefinite decades for ideal conditions; we need the understanding now. My Syracuse responsibilities are such that I must plan well in advance, in fact I could not have named 1950-51 if I had not started preliminary negotiations six months ago. The year 1952 is impractical since I shall have responsibilities for the International Geographical Congress, and 1953 is too long to wait. Professor Preston James is to be away in 1949-50, hence 1950-51 is the only feasible year.

III. Background and Publications

My initial contacts in China came in 1923 when I went to the Language School in Peiping, and then to the University of Shanghai. Following extensive travel I returned to the United States in 1929 and published "China's Geographic Foundations" in 1934. My interests then turned to the continent as a whole and especially to the Soviet Union. This resulted in "Asia's Lands and Peoples" in 1944 and "The Basis of Soviet Strength" in 1945.

I now propose to devote the coming decade to a reevaluation of China. The 1950-51 trip will be my fifth visit to Asia; I trust that it will be one of the most significant.

Academic positions are as follows:

1923-29		Assistant Professor, University of Shanghai
1931 to date		Professor of Geology and Geography, Syracuse University, and Chairman of the Department
1930-32	(summers)	Visiting Professor, Harvard
1937	(summer)	Visiting Professor, Western Reserve
1939	(summer)	Visiting Professor, Michigan
1941-44	(summers)	Visiting Professor, Columbia
1943-44		Visiting Professor in China, Department of State Cultural Relations Program
1945-46		Visiting Professor, Stanford University

My professional responsibilities have been rather extensive. The following list covers representative activities.

International Geographical Union - Vice-President since 1947 and Chairman of the U.S. National Committee (under National Research Council); Head of U.S. delegation to Lisbon Congress 1949.
National Research Council, Division of Geology and Geography, Chairman of numerous committees over several years.
Association of American Geographers - Councellor
Far Eastern Quarterly, Advisory Editor
American Slavic and East European Review, Editorial Board
Economic Geography, Associate Editor
American Institute of Pacific Relations, Trustee
Foreign Policy Association, Director

In the Asiatic field my total publication exceeds 1000 pages; the following titles include the principal contributions to Chinese geography.

China's Geographic Foundations (McGraw-Hill, New York, (1934); with Paris translation, Payot (1939).)
The Ordos Desert of Inner Mongolia (Denison University Bulletin, Journal of Scientific Laboratories, XXXIII, (1933), 155-248.)
The Land Forms of Chekiang (Annals, Association of American Geographers, XXVIII (1938), 259-276.)
Agricultural Regions of Asia, Part VI, China (Economic Geography, X (1934), 109-142.)
Foundations of Chinese Life (Economic Geography, XV (1939), 95-104.)
The Fenghsien Landscape (Geographical Review, XXVI (1936), 504-507.)
Asia's Lands and Peoples (McGraw-Hill, New York, (1944); with Spanish translation, Editorial Sudamericana, Buenos Aires, (1946); and Chinese translation, Commercial Press, Shanghai, (1946).)
The Basis of Soviet Strength (Whittlesey House, New York, (1945), London, (1946).)

George B. Cressey - 4

IV. Costs

The following budget can only be suggestive.

In my Fullbright application I have asked for funds to cover the following:
a) salary
b) purchase of publications in Chinese
c) an advanced Chinese student as field assistant and translator
d) secretarial aid
e) extensive travel within China
f) conferences with Chinese geographers
g) support for half a dozen advanced students from America

Syracuse University presumably will grant a leave on half salary, plus a research assistant in both 49-50 and 51-52, plus secretarial services and supplies. This would total about $9,000. It is also possible to secure books and other material from our departmental budget.

IF this application is limited to a travel grant to and from China to supplement Fullbright funds, the budget requested from S.S.R.C. is something as follows:

a) Rail and Pullman, Syracuse to San Francisco for our family of six @ $146.87 plus $20. incidentals, with return trip. (This would be reduced if we drove our car to the coast, but the saving would about equal shipping charges for the car across the Pacific)	$2,002,44
b) Trans Pacific round trip passage, @ $750. via "General"boats or $1,000. each via "President" boats (Rates a year hence are unpredictable)	4,500.00 to $6,000.00
c) Round trip transportation for six graduate students, say $1000. to $1300. each, or less if via rail coach and boat intermediate class.	5,500.00 to 7,000.00
	$10,000.00 to 15,000.00

On the above basis, the total project might involve some $40,000. depending on the size of the Fullbright stipend for the students. Only nominal parts of this total can be met from personal funds.